D1114608

CAWOOD'S COMMENTS

39 Years of Notes, Quotes and Anecdotes

Host Creative Communications
Lexington, Kentucky

"Cawood's Comments" is published and printed by Host Creative Communications, 904 North Broadway, Lexington, Kentucky 40505.

Edited by Tom Wallace, Brooks Downing, J.D. Rutledge, Ed Kromer
Layout by Michaela Ristich Duzyk
Cover Photography by Tony Leonard
Photography by Tony Leonard, David Coyle and
University of Kentucky Sports Communications

ISBN: 1-879688-09-3
(Second Printing)

I would like to dedicate this book to the countless University of Kentucky fans everywhere. Your loyalty, trust and support have made my 39 years as "Voice of the Wildcats" a rare and wonderful experience.

TABLE OF CONTENTS

NOTEBOOKS

UK BASKETBALL

UK FOOTBALL

BLUEGRASS PERSONALITIES

COMMENTS

AWARDS

INTRODUCTION

Shortly after I announced that this would be my final year of broadcasting University of Kentucky sports, Tom Wallace of my staff came to me with the idea for this book. After giving Tom's suggestion some thought, I found myself agreeing that it was a good idea.

It has been my privilege to be on hand for many great sporting events in my 39 years as "Voice of the Wildcats." I've been fortunate to know many of the people who fashioned Kentucky's rich sports tradition, both at UK and around the Commonwealth, whether it was on the basketball court, the football field or the race track.

That's what Cawood's Comments is about...the great sporting events that have become part of our history, and the many memorable characters who breathed life into those events.

Doing a book of this nature is fun, but it's no easy undertaking. There were 3,000 manuscripts dating back more than a dozen years that had to be sifted through. There were interviews and programs that were recorded many years ago. We had to go through those tapes, listen to them, then decide what we needed and didn't need. These tapes were originally presented as Cawood's Comments, Cawood's Notebooks or Conversation with Cawood that aired on radio or television stations across the state.

As you can see, there certainly was no shortage of material to choose from. That meant Tom, Brooks Downing and I were faced with the difficult task of deciding which ones to include and which ones to leave out. That's about like trying to decide which Wildcat player is your all-time favorite. No matter which ones you pick — or how many — you're invariably going to leave out some good ones. But we simply couldn't use all 3,000 scripts, and I hope you agree that we have selected the best ones.

I know you'll enjoy reading again about Adolph Rupp's first visit to Lexington, and how his initial impression of Kentucky was less than favorable. And how Ed Diddle hit upon the idea for his trademark red towel that he waved triumphantly when his great Western Kentucky University teams were on their way to another win. It was fun getting Howard Schnellenberger, now the successful coach at Louisville, to remember his days as an All-American at UK and the touchdown pass he caught to beat Tennessee. There's the story of Secretariat, perhaps the greatest race horse that ever lived, and the incredible Cinderella story of Judy Hicks, who bought a horse for $10 at a sheriff's sale and saw it go on to win almost $1 million.

And these stories are just the tip of the iceberg. There are many, many more that touch on virtually every area of the sports world and the people who make up that world.

An undertaking such as this couldn't be accomplished without the superhuman efforts of many people. I would like to thank Tom and Brooks for shaping the direction of this book. I want to thank Kim Ramsay, Rebecca Bach and Andrea Marshall for the many hours they spent staring at a computer screen while transposing the spoken word to the page. And, finally, a big thanks to Rick Ford, J.D. Rutledge, Ed Kromer, Michaela Duzyk and the rest of the folks in sports publishing at Host Creative Communications for making the final product look so good.

But most of all, I want to thank you wonderful fans for allowing me to serve as the link between the action on the playing fields and your living room. It has been a memorable journey for me, and I hope, through this book, I was able to share many of these experiences with you.

I hope you enjoy it.

Cawood Ledford

CAWOOD'S
NOTEBOOKS

HIS NAME WAS ADOLPH RUPP

(Adolph Rupp won more games at the University of Kentucky than any other coach in college basketball history. His final record at UK after 42 seasons was 875-190. But did you know that the "Baron" was something less than impressed with UK and Lexington when he made his first visit?)

LEDFORD: Almost every great sports tradition began with a single individual. Notre Dame's incredible football tradition had its beginning when Knute Rockne became the coach of the Fighting Irish. The New York Yankees established their famous baseball tradition when Babe Ruth pulled on the pin stripes and belted the ball out of Yankee Stadium. The University of Kentucky's unrivaled basketball tradition was no different. It had its beginning in 1930, when a 30-year-old Kansas native arrived on the UK campus.

His name was Adolph Rupp.

In 1930, the UK athletics department had a heavy Illinois influence. Athletics director Daddy Boles, football coach Harry Gamage and basketball coach Johnny Mauer were all Illinois men. When Mauer left for Miami of Ohio at the end of that season, UK's leaders naturally looked to Illinois for a replacement. At the time, a young coach at Freeport High School was making quite a record for himself, and the young coach's success didn't go unnoticed by the UK hierarchy.

His name was Adolph Rupp.

RUPP: "I got a telegram from Daddy Boles, who was the athletic director, inviting me to come down here to apply for the job."

LEDFORD: Rupp wasn't at all sure he was interested in leaving a top high school position for a university he knew little about. However, the lure of a free trip was too much for Rupp to turn down.

RUPP: "I wasn't too hot to come down here at the time, but I thought I'd come down and look at it. It was a free trip with expenses paid. And, of course, that was something worth looking into."

LEDFORD: Rupp was met at the depot by the UK contingent, then taken on a tour through one of the worst parts of Lexington. Shanties and tarpaper shacks lined the streets. To make matters worse, after the tour, they took Rupp to the school cafeteria for a lunch consisting of leftovers.

RUPP: "They had run out of everything but some cold fish, and each of us had a corn stick. That's all we had for lunch. So when I left here, I thought I wasn't too sure that the residential section of this town was too inviting or that the meals were too outstanding."

LEDFORD: While Rupp was in Lexington, the UK committee asked him about the style of play he planned to use if he did get the job. Rupp, who was never short on answers, was only too happy to tell them.

RUPP: "Well, they finally grilled me about basketball. How was basketball going to be any different under me than it was under this other coach? I told them about our style, how we liked to run, and how we liked to rebound, how we liked to shoot, and how we liked to get that ball off the board, and if we didn't have the fast break, then we'd go into a definite pattern offense."

LEDFORD: Although Rupp's fast-break style of play was contrary to the style of that day, he didn't back down. Instead, he stuck to his guns.

RUPP: "I like to give people action. If they didn't want any action, they didn't want me."

LEDFORD: There were 70 candidates for the coaching position, but in the end, the UK group saw something in Rupp they liked. He got the job, and the rest is, as they say, history. Rupp would go on to win more games than any coach who ever lived. Rupp was a notoriously superstitious man. He had more superstitions than you could count. One of his most famous, the one that earned him the nickname "The Man in the Brown Suit," was one he brought with him to the Bluegrass State.

RUPP: "I had an old suit when I started coaching and it got kind of thin. It was a brown suit, and it just happened to be brown I guess because it's the cheapest thing I could buy at the time. Finally, I got a new suit — cost me $22.50, I remember that — and it was blue. I thought it was time to change the color, so that night I made a very auspicious entry into the gymnasium in my new suit. I don't think anybody noticed it. And we got clobbered! So I got to studying about that thing and I figured that new suit didn't help me any. I got the old brown suit out again and we started winning. From that time on, I have never been in anything except a brown suit on the day of a game."

LEDFORD: The University of Kentucky's school colors are blue and white, but its great basketball tradition was started by a young man who wore nothing but brown suits.

His name was Adolph Rupp.

Legendary Kentucky coach Adolph Rupp's credentials were impressive — 875 wins, four national championships, one National Invitation Tournament title and 27 SEC crowns.

REMEMBERING THE BARON

(There are enough Adolph Rupp stories to fill a 10-volume collection of books. Everyone, it seems, has a favorite Rupp story, including former Wildcats Wallace "Wah Wah" Jones, Louie Dampier and Vernon Hatton, who joined me recently to remember the Baron.)

LEDFORD: Adolph Rupp coached the Kentucky Wildcats for 42 years. To this day, Adolph Rupp stories are often the topic of conversation whenever UK fans gather. Or when his former players gather. Wallace "Wah Wah" Jones was a member of The Fabulous Five in the late '40s. One of Wah's favorite stories took place at Alabama.

JONES: "They shot a gun off at halftime and they threw a big stuffed bird out on the floor while you were running down the floor, like they shot it out of the air. And they'd throw money out on the floor when things were going bad. Rupp knew this was going to happen, so he made a speech in the dressing room and told all of us in there, 'Now, I don't want you to let this upset you, but they're going to throw this money. Don't pick up anything, just go ahead and shoot your shots.' Shively, our athletics director, was out of the room at the time, so we come in and they're sitting on the bench. Rupp is at one end and Shive's at the other end when this money started falling all over the place. Here would come a dime or a nickle down through there and nobody ever touched it. Finally, a quarter rolled across in front of the bench and Shively reached out and grabbed it. Adolph looked down the bench and said, 'Well, Shive, I see they've met your price.' "

LEDFORD: 'Shive' was Bernie Shively, the long-time athletics director at UK. Louie Dampier was an All-American on the 1966 Rupp's Runts, and one of his favorite Rupp stories also involved the former Wildcat AD.

DAMPIER: "After our Runts' year, we represented the United States in a world tournament over in Israel. After the tournament, which we won, we all marched in, more or less like the Olympics, and stood there as they raised the flags. They played every nation's anthem. I was right beside Mr. Shively and Coach Rupp was next to him. They were playing all the anthems but we never heard ours. Coach Rupp leaned over and said, 'Shive, I didn't hear them play our anthem. Did they?' And Shive said, 'Well, Coach, you didn't recognize it because they played it in Hebrew.' "

LEDFORD: Another UK All-American is Vernon Hatton, captain of the NCAA championship team in 1958. Hatton made one of the most famous shots in UK basketball history, firing one up from midcourt with one second to go as UK won a three-overtime thriller against Temple.

HATTON: "After I'd made the one-second shot, I decided to go in and visit Coach Rupp the next morning and ask him for the game ball. I knocked on the door, went in — I was kind of excited — and said, 'Co..Co..Coach Rupp, could I have the ga..game ball from last night?' He said, 'Why in the hell should I give you the game ball? If it hadn't been you who took that shot, I'd have let somebody else shoot it and they would have made it. I can't justify giving you a $35 game ball just because you made two points.' Well, I got all excited and was about ready to walk out when he said, 'Hey, Hatton, here's the ball. Keep it and show it to your grandchildren one of these days.' And I've done that. And I've always admired him for doing that. He had the ball there ready to give to me."

LEDFORD: Adolph Rupp stories have remained popular through the years. And that's not likely to change.

THE GOSPEL ACCORDING TO THE BARON

(Adolph Rupp was one of the funniest, wittiest men I have ever had the privilege of being around. What follows are several Notebooks in which the legendary coach reminisced about his days at UK.)

LEDFORD: Adolph Frederick Rupp coached the Kentucky basketball team for 42 years. He retired following the 1972 season. He died in 1977. But let's turn back the clock, back to when Rupp was still coaching. For starters, let's ask Rupp what he looked for in a prospective Wildcat.

RUPP: "You look for quick reaction. You look, of course, for size if you can get it, although some of our best athletes here at the University were not big men. And then, of course, you also look for the reaction of the boy. The thing you can't tell about a boy is his heart. Will he go to war when the time demands?"

LEDFORD: Rupp's players went to war when the time demanded. That's why he won more games than any coach who ever lived. Yet, everytime Rupp sent a team out to face an opponent, he worried about the outcome.

RUPP: "I regard everybody as a worthy opponent. I regard them that way. I'm scared to death, and I have been for 42 years, since I've been here. Even though I felt sure that we were going to win, I still ran scared."

LEDFORD: So did Kentucky's opponents. Each season, the first goal on Coach Rupp's agenda was winning the Southeastern Conference. He won that championship 27 times. He even had the formula for achieving that goal.

RUPP: "To start with, you have to win all of your home games...let's just put that down first. Then you have to win a majority of games away from home. And then you have to win the close games."

LEDFORD: In 42 years, the cast of players changed many times under Adolph Rupp. Those teams varied greatly in ability too. But the Rupp stamp never varied. You could always count on seeing a good-shooting team that played an up-tempo fast-breaking style of basketball.

RUPP: "As long as you shoot well, as long as you run well, as long as you rebound well, as long as you run, you're going to have a good basketball team."

LEDFORD: Adolph Rupp was 70 when he coached his last Kentucky team. He realized, at the end of that campaign, he would be forced to retire. Yet even to the very end, he never lost his great competitive fire.

RUPP: "Cawood, every game is just the same as the first game. I certainly do get a kick out of it, and whenever you fail to get a kick out of the things that you're doing, you ought to change and do something else. I just like to take a bunch of boys and put them out there on the floor and try to beat somebody if I possibly can."

LEDFORD: After the 1972 season, the Adolph Rupp Era was over at Kentucky. In 1976, the building that bears his name was dedicated. He died the following year.

REMEMBRANCES OF RUPP

(In this series, we're reminiscing about the late Adolph Rupp...the man who built Kentucky's great basketball tradition. Boston Celtics' general manager Red Auerbach once said that he would rather watch Kentucky practice than to watch most teams play. As I remember the UK practice sessions when Adolph Rupp was the coach, they were short, silent and intense. The players came to practice and shot free throws on their own. At exactly 3:15, each player began a 30-minute shooting drill. After that, it became serious business.)

RUPP: "It's been described by some people that our practice is run in a military fashion, but that isn't the case. I want to run every practice session so that my boys understand exactly what we're trying to do that particular day."

LEDFORD: Rupp's practice sessions were famous for their silence. There was absolutely no talking by the players. The only sounds that came out of Memorial Coliseum were the bouncing balls and the screeching of rubber soles on a hardwood floor. And there was no wasted time. Each day, Coach Rupp had the practice planned down to the smallest detail.

RUPP: "I call the boys together and tell them exactly what we're going to do. We don't go out there and laugh and holler and make a lot of noise and things like that, the way you see some teams do that are very disorganized. I want everything organized and I want it sound fundamentally. If you've got a sound fundamental ballclub, they're being serious somewhere along the way."

LEDFORD: Coach Rupp believed that the discipline and the sacrifices a player made at Kentucky would make that person stronger and better prepared to face life after basketball. Why?

RUPP: "Because I don't believe that you can get anything better in this world than to take a bunch of boys and put them in competition and see them succeed."

LEDFORD: In all those years on the Kentucky bench, it was inevitable that Rupp would have his share of run-ins with the men in the striped shirts. After losing once in New York, he questioned the officiating by paraphrasing the Bible, saying "I was a stranger and they took me in." Rupp actually did some high school officiating during his early days at Kentucky, and he often looked back humorously to those days when was a member of the refereeing tribe.

RUPP: "The idea of officiating is to keep the game going. Whenever I officiated a ballgame, I always figured how much money do I get for this and then tried to earn it as fast as I could. And I got on the road as fast as I could get going."

LEDFORD: He also could get right to the point when he was unhappy with the officiating, as he did in a post-game show after a tough battle on the road.

RUPP: "I'll tell you one thing...we had six fouls before you could say 'Scat' out there tonight. We had five at the end of four minutes, and I just thought they (officials) had been sent in here by the Communists to blow us out of the place."

LEDFORD: Adolph Rupp's teams seldom were blown out of any place, yet he never let the chance go by to let the officials know they might have done a better job. Rupp may have once been an official, but that didn't mean he had to like them.

THE RUPP PHILOSOPHY AND SUPERSTITIONS

(For the past two Notebooks, we've featured the late Adolph Rupp. We conclude the series by taking a look at some of Rupp's philosophies and superstitions.)

LEDFORD: During his 42-year coaching career, Adolph Rupp was tagged with several monickers. "Old Rupp and Ready" and "The Baron of Basketball" were among them, but the alias that really stuck was "The Man in the Brown Suit." While still coaching high school basketball in Freeport, Ill., Rupp had become convinced that wearing a brown suit at his games had brought him success. He never wore anything else. He also looked for hair pins on the day of a game. The more he found, the better he felt about his team's chances that night. He parked in the same spot for every home game. He stepped on the same manhole cover. He crossed the street at exactly the same place. While some called them superstitions, Rupp preferred to call it something else...luck.

RUPP: "If you're honest, if you're successful, luck has been on your side. I've carried a four-leaf clover and a buckeye in my pocket for years."

LEDFORD: Whatever it was, superstition or luck, Adolph Rupp had the magic for winning basketball games. More than magic, luck or superstition, Rupp was driven. He talked often about success. In the world of college basketball, he believed the only way to measure success was to count up the wins. He counted more of them than any man who ever coached. And he never felt the need to apologize for winning.

RUPP: "I don't believe that I've held my job here at the University with the idea in mind that our alumni and our student body didn't care whether we won or lost around here."

LEDFORD: To this day, many Kentuckians live and die with Kentucky basketball. Adolph Rupp gave them teams that won — and excelled — for more than 40 years. Anytime you wanted to turn Rupp's blood pressure up a few notches, all you had to do was recite Grantland Rice's famous poem. "When the One Great Scorer comes to write against your name, it matters not that you won or lost, but how you played the game."

RUPP: "If it doesn't make any difference, why put scoreboards up there? Why keep score? Why, it makes all the difference in the world."

LEDFORD: Perhaps that's why, under Adolph Rupp's guidance, the Wildcats won over 82 percent of their games. He long since has been enshrined in the Basketball Hall of Fame. His teams won four NCAA championships, an NIT title, an Olympic Gold Medal. We've enjoyed reminiscing about the great coach this week. Adolph F. Rupp. Born in Halstead, Kansas, he was a Kentuckian through and through when he died in 1977.

Rupp-coached UK teams won 82 percent of their games.

THE FABULOUS FIVE

(Alex Groza, Ralph Beard, Wah Jones, Cliff Barker, Kenny Rollins...Kentucky Wildcat fans learn those names before they learn the presidents. They were the fabled Fabulous Five, and even today, more than 40 years after they played, many still consider them to be UK's greatest basketball team.)

LEDFORD: Adolph Rupp had enjoyed more than a decade of success at the University of Kentucky, but it wasn't until the end of World War II that the journey down what the Baron would later call "The Glory Road" began. At the heart of that journey lies the 1947-48 team...The Fabulous Five. And at the heart of that team was Beard, the fiery three-time All-American and one of the greatest Wildcats ever. According to Beard, the success of that team, which had been shaped by the war, wasn't surprising.

BEARD: "I think it was the ingredients of The Fabulous Five...we had youth in Wah Wah Jones and myself, we had the veterans in Groza, Rollins and Barker, who had all played service ball. They were 24 to 27 years of age. Then you mix that with the coaching ability of Coach Rupp and I think that's what made The Fabulous Five."

LEDFORD: The Fabulous Five finished with a 36-3 record. They waltzed through the NCAA tournament, then went to England and helped the United States win the (Olympic) gold medal in basketball. It was such a dominant team, and one blessed with so much talent that competition in practice often surpassed the competition faced in regular-season games. Beard is quick to agree.

BEARD: "They were the best games that we played in. The first and second teams would go at each other, and a lot of times, I've got to admit this now, a lot of times the second team would be ahead at the end of regulation. Coach Rupp would say Humzey (Yessin), who was the referee, he'd say let's go another three minutes. And so the starters would finally get up, and then Coach Rupp would say that's it. But, I'm telling you, those practices were war, and they really made us better."

LEDFORD: From its earliest beginnings, basketball had been a slow-motion sport. The wily Rupp, however, would have no part of that. He turned things up several notches by introducing the run-and-gun style. Still, it wasn't until he unleashed The Fabulous Five that college basketball was brought face to face with the future.

BEARD: "It was even written back then that we had sort of changed the game even though, at that time, they had Rhode Island State, which had what was called a fire-engine brand of basketball. But ours was a controlled fast-break. We always took it when we had it. We also pressed end-to-end some, so, yes, I would say that that was the start of modern-day basketball."

LEDFORD: The Fabulous Five is without question the University of Kentucky's most legendary team. Some say it's still UK's best, even though more than 40 years have passed since they played. Forty years and still the measuring stick for all UK teams. That may be the ultimate testimony to their greatness.

BEARD: "We all had the same goal...to be the national champions and the best that we could be. I think that's what spurred us on."

WAH WAH

(Wah Wah Jones is arguably the most-versatile athlete to ever wear the blue and white at Kentucky. He starred in football, baseball and basketball at UK during the late 1940s. Despite his all-around talent, he is perhaps best known for being a part of Adolph Rupp's Fabulous Five.)

LEDFORD: Who were UK's Fabulous Five? It's an often-asked question around Kentucky. Ralph Beard, Kenny Rollins, Alex Groza, Cliff Barker and Wah Jones made up the starting team. From 1946 through 1949, The Fabulous Five won an NIT championship, two NCAA titles and an Olympic gold medal. Harlan native Wah Jones says it seemed the wins just kept on coming.

JONES: "In the four years I was there, we won the NIT and were runner-up the next year. Then we came back the next two years and won the NCAA. So the four years that Beard and I played together, I think we won 130 games out of 140."

LEDFORD: The Fabulous Five were noted for their great precision. Each player had a specialty on that team. Rollins was the quarterback on the floor. Barker was an exceptional passer. Beard was known for his deadly shot. But according to Wah, Beard was more than a scorer. He was a defensive stopper as well.

JONES: "Ralph, as you know, was a real defensive player, plus a very good offensive player. Coach Rupp would send him to guard a guy and he hardly would let him out of his sight. Coach Rupp once told Beard to go up in the stands and sit with his man if he moved up there."

LEDFORD: Groza was the center on that team, one of the best Wildcat centers of all-time. He could crash the boards and score with the best of them.

JONES: "He had the great touch, a good hook shot, and he worked very well in the pivot. His hands, on tipping the ball, he had great touch there. He could tip it back up and put a spin on it and get it in the goal."

LEDFORD: Wah was the team's down-in-the-trenches battler. Beard liked to call him the "enforcer." Wah was named All-American his senior year, and probably would have been made All-American the two previous years had he concentrated strictly on basketball. Run-and-gun basketball, that is, which was the Wildcats' trademark style of play.

JONES: "Well, we didn't hardly believe in the dribble. We moved it down the floor real fast. I'd get the ball out under the basket a lot of times just as soon as it went through and throw it out to midcourt almost. And we'd take off from there. We did get down the floor real quick."

LEDFORD: When Rupp was being interviewed for the UK coaching job, he told the hiring committee that if they wanted a ball-control game, he wasn't their man. He said his teams were going to push the ball up the floor. The Fabulous Five pushed it up and down the floor better than anyone, on its way to becoming one of the legendary teams in college basketball history.

THE CAPTAIN

(Kenny Rollins had one of the most celebrated careers in University of Kentucky basketball history. He captained the great Fabulous Five NCAA championship team in 1948, and he won an Olympic gold medal later that same year.)

LEDFORD: Cliff Barker, Ralph Beard, Wah Jones, Alex Groza, Kenny Rollins...The Fabulous Five. Their names are at the heart of UK's success story. Kenny Rollins, the man who captained that special, talent-rich team, knows why it enjoyed such huge success.

ROLLINS: "What made our team so great, I think one of the many things, is that we not only had good shooters and strength and speed and quickness, but we had two guys that were willing to sacrifice their points in order to feed the others. Normally you'll have one fellow on a ballclub willing to do that. One fellow willing to be the passer. We had two, and I think that's one of the many reasons we were so successful. It's the same reason Rupp's Runts were so successful. Tommy Kron and Larry Conley were willing to feed."

LEDFORD: One year later, in 1949, the Wildcats repeated as NCAA champs. Yet, despite the presence of four returning starters from the previous year, Ralph Beard says the '49 team wasn't as good. And the reason why, Ralph says, is because the '49 club didn't have Kenny Rollins.

ROLLINS: "Well, I don't know that I agree with Ralph. I think that the second year, the year after I was gone, was just as good. But it took a little while to find the guy to take my place. Eventually, what they did was move Cliff Barker from a forward back to a guard."

LEDFORD: Like almost every athlete who has been fortunate enough to win an Olympic gold medal, Rollins ranks that as his greatest moment in athletics. He remembers.

ROLLINS: "An experience I will never forget, to be standing on that podium, be presented your gold medal and hear the National Anthem, and know that you're playing for your country. Chill bumps ran all over me. I was almost numb when it was all over with. I couldn't move for just a few seconds."

LEDFORD: Rollins played for the legendary Adolph Rupp. These days, he watches Rick Pitino calling the shots from the sidelines. Rollins sees great similarities between the two men.

ROLLINS: "I see terrific, tremendous dedication to the game. A continual student of the game. A disciplinarian with a strong feeling and support for the boys that are playing for him. A man who helps his players understand that what they are doing is to continue the tradition that we feel we started."

LEDFORD: Yes, Kenny, you and your Fabulous Five teammates started one of the great traditions in all of sports. And all Wildcat fans thank you for laying that foundation.

ALEX THE GREAT

(There are many who still maintain that Alex Groza is the greatest center to ever play basketball for the University of Kentucky. He was a three-time All-American, twice the NCAA Tournament's MVP, a member of The Fabulous Five and the school's all-time leading scorer when he left.)

LEDFORD: Alex Groza came to Kentucky from the steel mills of Ohio, and by the time he left after the 1949 season, he had forever etched his name into the Wildcat record books. He had been at the center of a team many still rank as UK's greatest...The Fabulous Five. Why was that team so spectacularly successful? Groza says a lot of it had to do with togetherness.

GROZA: "From the standpoint of playing together for so long, I think it made us a much better basketball team than if changes were made, mass changes every year. We got to know one another's moves, one another's actions. We could help one another. We knew their strong points, their weaknesses, and I think it helped all of us be better basketball players and a better basketball team."

LEDFORD: The Fabulous Five was not only UK's greatest team, it was also the one credited with ushering in today's modern-style game. But The Fabulous Five wasn't just a team molded by Adolph Rupp...it was a team shaped by fate and destiny.

GROZA: "That's right, Cliff Barker was a granddaddy when he came here somewhere back in '39 or '40. He went into the service and was a prisoner of war. Kenny came, then he also went into the service, the Navy for two or three years. When I came, I went into the Army for two years. In the meantime,

Wah Wah and Ralph came. Now when the war was over, we all came back and we all got together on the same basketball team. As fate would have it, that was a golden era, I think, of collegiate sports all through the country. But the better athletes came back to Kentucky."

LEDFORD: Those Wildcat teams were so talent-rich, so dominant, that the regular-season games were little more than public workouts. The real battles, those veterans will tell you, took place during practice.

GROZA: "Adolph had 18 guys on that basketball team that could play basketball. When we scrimmaged in practice, the second team oft-times got the best of the first team. So whether he started the first team or second team, I think Adolph would have had a great basketball team and a great career and great record."

LEDFORD: Down through the years, UK has had a host of great pivot men. Bill Spivey, Cliff Hagan, Dan Issel, Sam Bowie...the record books are filled with their impressive numbers. Yet none stood taller than Alex Groza. He was the first great one, the one who set the standard by which all others will forever be judged.

HUMZEY THE HELPER

(Between 1945 and 1949, the Kentucky Wildcat basketball teams won two NCAA championships, an NIT title and an Olympic gold medal while recording a 130-10 record. Among the Wildcats was one of the most popular managers ever at Kentucky...Humzey Yessin.)

LEDFORD: Humzey Yessin was the popular team manager during The Fabulous Five years. He later served as a scout for Coach Adolph Rupp. Yessin fondly recalls The Fabulous Five of Alex Groza, Ralph Beard, Wah Jones, Cliff Barker and Kenny Rollins.

YESSIN: "The publicity that The Fabulous Five got during those years was just outstanding. And they were, you know, clean-cut all-American boys that everybody identified with. The community loved them and the state loved them. They were nationally known and internationally known."

LEDFORD: According to Humzey, the toughest part of playing for the Wildcats was making the team. One year, at least 30 players tried out for the Cats, including freshmen, returning servicemen from World War II and walk-ons. Humzey says the competition was fierce.

YESSIN: "In fact, one year a 12-man squad going to the Southeastern Conference left off two All-Americans. No, make that three All-Americans. Bob Brannum, Jim Jordan and Jack Parkinson did not make the traveling squad."

LEDFORD: During the '50s, Yessin served as scout for Coach Rupp. That wasn't the easiest of jobs, either. Humzey remembered one occasion when some advice that he, Baldy Gilb and Buddy Parker gave to Rupp backfired. It was against

Dayton in the 1955 UKIT championship game.

YESSIN: "They had about a 10- or 12-point lead on us at halftime. We came back out the second half and we were just exchanging baskets with them. Coach Rupp turned around and said, 'Have you guys got anything?' So Buddy Parker says, 'Coach, we're going to have to pick them up.' Baldy Gilb nodded like he usually did. Then Coach Rupp says, 'What do you think, Hum?' I says, 'Coach, we've gotta pick them up, we're just swapping baskets.' "

LEDFORD: Coach Rupp called timeout immediately and put the full court press on. Dayton was ready, and almost instantly the Flyers' lead went from 10 points to 22 points in a matter of minutes. Dayton went on to win 89-74. The next day Humzey was sure Coach Rupp would blame him for the loss. Rupp called Humzey to the Coliseum.

YESSIN: "When I walked into Memorial Coliseum, Coach Rupp was sitting there going over the shot chart. He said, 'Well, we were playing the nation's No. 1 club to about a 10- to 12-point game until I got some fool advice from three son-of-a-bucks behind our bench.' "

LEDFORD: Coach Rupp didn't blame the loss on Humzey Yessin. Instead, the Baron presented the Harlan native with a tournament watch, stating, "There's enough glory for all of us, Humzey."

PERFECT NON-CHAMPS

(The 1953-54 Kentucky Wildcats finished with a perfect 25-0 record, yet did not participate in the NCAA tournament because "The Big Three" of Cliff Hagan, Frank Ramsey and Lou Tsioropoulos, graduate students at the time, were declared ineligible because of a then-NCAA rule barring post-graduates from participating in the NCAA tournament.)

LEDFORD: It is the most unique team in NCAA basketball history...the only team ever to go undefeated and not win the national championship. It is also one of UK's greatest teams. In a recent book, CBS basketball analyst Billy Packer ranked the 1953-54 Wildcats as the fifth-best college basketball team in history. And with good reason. Those Wildcats gunned down 25-straight opponents with machine-like precision. The closest anyone could get to them was six points. Included among their victims was LaSalle, the eventual NCAA champion. Frank Ramsey was an All-American guard on that UK team, and he says the reason for the Cats' success was simple.

RAMSEY: "I think the first thing was we had an experienced team. The year before (1952-53) we had not been able to play at all. All we did that year was practice. We had three post-graduate students, we had about four seniors, and then there were about 12 freshmen that came in. So when the following season came around, which was the '54 season, we were prepared."

LEDFORD: The 1953-54 team was led by "The Big Three"...Ramsey, All-American Cliff Hagan and Lou Tsioropoulos. The previous season, UK was on NCAA probation and not allowed to play, so when the forced exile ended in 1953, Adolph Rupp had his team polished like shiny silver.

RAMSEY: "That particular season, we wanted to go undefeated and prove that we had been wronged, because when Kentucky was put on probation for that one year, it was for events that happened while we were all still in high school. I think that we just wanted to win, and we would do just about anything possible to win."

LEDFORD: Fueled by the Baron's sense of vengeance, and led by the great Hagan-Ramsey duo, the '53-54 Wildcats easily blitzed through their schedule. The tipoff to just how good that team was can be found in the 73-60 win over LaSalle in the first UKIT. Although Ramsey won't come out and say the Wildcats would have won the NCAA title, it's clear that he would have liked his team's chances.

RAMSEY: "Well, it's hard to say. In order to win the NCAA tournament, you have to have no injuries, you have to win the close games and you have to have a lot of luck. I would have liked to thought that we would have fared extremely well had we been allowed to play."

LEDFORD: That the '53-54 Wildcats were barred from post-season play is one of the great injustices in college sports history. And that injustice becomes even more pronounced when you consider why UK was banned. What happened was UK was penalized because "The Big Three" had done the job where it counts the most — in the classroom.

RAMSEY: "At that time, there was a rule in the NCAA that said if you were a graduate student and are to receive your degree, you could not play at any post-season events. We were all in graduate school, which meant that we were not allowed to play because we had progressed toward a degree in a timely manner."

LEDFORD: The 1953-54 UK team is one of the best I've

ever seen, and surely Hagan and Ramsey are among UK's most glittering stars. It's a tragedy they weren't allowed to participate in the NCAA tournament. Clearly, the best dancers weren't invited to the big ball. And because of that, we are left to wonder what might have been.

The 1953-54 Wildcats, led by graduate student Frank Ramsey, roared to a perfect 25-0 season, but were not allowed to participate in the NCAA tournament.

RUPP'S RUNTS

(Rupp's Runts remain one of UK's most cherished teams. That 1965-66 unit rose from nowhere to reach the No. 1 ranking in the nation, eventually advancing to the NCAA championship game, where it lost to Texas Western 72-65. Larry Conley, a senior that season, was the glue that held the club together.)

LEDFORD: Four starters were back from a team that was only so-so at best the prior season. The tallest starter was a guard. So there was little reason for optimism among the UK faithful as the 1965-66 campaign rolled around. However, as things turned out, everyone was in for a pleasant surprise, because that team ran off 23 straight wins, finished the season with a 27-2 record and second-place in the NCAA Tournament. These were Rupp's Runts...perhaps the most popular team in Kentucky's storied basketball history.

When the 1965 Wildcats began the season, they were ranked nowhere...not on anybody's top anything list. Unlike most UK teams, nothing much was expected. Tommy Kron and Larry Conley were the seniors on that team and they were far from satisfied with the way things were shaping up. They both knew that something needed to be done, so Larry says he and Tommy made a decision.

CONLEY: "We needed to do something to make this a better team. And we kind of decided to give up our scoring and pick up what we could do from the standpoint of making the team a better club. I mean, I was a scorer in high school. So was Tom Kron, yet the fact that we were willing to give that up and maybe make some sacrifices in a couple of areas made us a lot better club."

LEDFORD: That's what happened. Kron and Conley sacrificed themselves for the good of the club. Louie Dampier and

Pat Riley were the chief beneficiaries...both made first-team All-American. Thad Jaracz made third-team All-American. While Kron and Conley were at the heart of the Runts' success, another key factor was the team's fast start. Six quick wins helped the undersized, unranked Wildcats begin to believe in themselves.

CONLEY: "I really think the turnaround game for us was Texas Tech, out in Lubbock. That's when we really discovered we were pretty good, because we'd gone into that game and we were down at halftime. We went to the one-three-one and they didn't score a field goal for nine and a half minutes. And all of a sudden we started looking around, and I said, 'Hey, we're pretty good, we can play this game.' "

LEDFORD: Twenty-three straight wins and a No. 1 ranking. Yes, that team could play the game. But Kentucky has had many fine teams over the years, including seven that finished the season ranked No. 1. What was it about the Runts that made them something special?

CONLEY: "I think a lot of fans in the state of Kentucky had begun to have visions of maybe Coach Rupp losing his control over the program, and perhaps that, you know, he was starting downhill, because he'd had the bad year the previous year and it looked as if the next year our club in '66 was not gonna be a very good team. I think there were visions of people saying, 'Oh, my goodness, he's losing it,' and I think maybe as we began to win, with each succeeding win, everybody felt better, that maybe Coach Rupp was going to be all right."

LEDFORD: That team was special to Coach Rupp. As long as he lived, he would never name his best player or best team, but he never failed to name his favorite team...Rupp's Runts. The Runts could have been one of the greatest Cinderella stories in history, but Texas Western spoiled the ending by upsetting the Cats in the NCAA finals. It was a crushing defeat, one that left Wildcat fans from Ashland to Paducah heartbroken. Their beloved Runts had come close only to miss out on the big prize. Back in Lexington on that March day in 1966, a tearful Larry Conley spoke to the 7,000 fans in Memorial Coliseum.

CONLEY: (After the game) "I'm just real sorry we couldn't bring back the big one, and I guess I can speak for all of us, because, ah, well, we went out there and tried. And that's about it. (Applause)

(Today) "Oh, I still think about it. If there's one thing in my whole life I could change, I'd want to change that game. I really wanted that game."

LEDFORD: Memories of Rupp's Runts will always remain bittersweet...a happy story with a sad ending. Yet, neither that loss to Texas Western nor the passing years have diminished their appeal or the special place they hold in the hearts of Wildcat fans. To this day, a quarter of a century later, Rupp's Runts are still perhaps the most popular team in Kentucky basketball history.

A ROLE-PLAYING HERO

(Every good basketball team has to have role players. Never was the importance of role players more apparent than during the 1965-66 season when Tommy Kron and Larry Conley sacrificed their own glory for the glory of the team.)

LEDFORD: Twenty-five years after a season that saw the Wildcats rise from mediocrity to stardom, Rupp's Runts are still famous. At a recent celebration at Rupp Arena honoring the group, the Runts received a standing ovation from the sellout crowd. But outside of the flashy Pat Riley and ace shooter Louie Dampier, the team consisted of role players. One was senior guard Tommy Kron.

KRON: "On the offensive end, I was the person who got the play started. I set picks, and also I was to go to the offensive board. That was my responsibility, but there were certain games where I had to do some shooting. Maybe they were playing the zone and my position was open and I was to take the shot. And then on the defensive end, I was to guard, generally, their high-scoring person, particularly a guard or forward. Occasionally, I even guarded a few centers, but we'd normally play a zone if we had a Clyde Lee to play against or someone like that. But it was my responsibility to take that guy and then, of course, on the zone, on the one-three-one that we played, the point position on that, that's pretty well defined."

LEDFORD: As one of two seniors, Kron had to provide much-needed guidance on the court to the young, but talented underclassmen.

KRON: "I felt I was a leader. I felt that my job was to get people who were down up, and when we had momentum to keep it going and make sure nobody let up...that we kept doing the things that we were doing well."

LEDFORD: It's obvious even today that the Runts still remember what it took to create a winning combination. But this was a team that rose from relative obscurity to become a national power. Kron said it's difficult to remember the moment when the players stopped and said, "Hey, we've got a real good team here."

KRON: "When we got to be about 8-0, around Christmas, all of a sudden we got in the Top 20. We weren't picked very high and then suddenly we're there. Then, of course, people, the writers, everyone got on the bandwagon pretty quick. When we got into the SEC and started winning every game, it picked up momentum."

LEDFORD: Kron's memory is right on the money. The Cats were 8-0 on Dec. 29, right after drilling Notre Dame 103-69. The team would not lose a game all year until March 5, when it was beaten on the road by archrival Tennessee 69-62. Its only other defeat came to Texas Western in the NCAA championship game. The Runts were a crowd favorite then, and the Runts are a crowd favorite now, 25 years later.

RILES' SIGNIFICANCE

(Pat Riley has become one of the most famous basketball Wildcats to ever graduate from Kentucky. The former Rupp's Runt is known across the nation for coaching the NBA's Los Angeles Lakers to four world championships. This fall, he takes over as the New York Knicks' coach.)

LEDFORD: When the University of Kentucky held a 25th-anniversary celebration not long ago for Rupp's Runts, it marked Pat Riley's first visit to Rupp Arena. Riley, of course, had a pretty good reason for his long absence from the UK scene. He's been tied up coaching the Lakers for nine great years. Riley, who has seen it all, was impressed by the arena and the Wildcat faithful.

RILEY: "It's a pretty raucous crowd, but I'd bet you they'd be a little more raucous if Dale Brown was here with LSU."

LEDFORD: Rick Pitino invited Riley to speak to the UK team before going out to face Tennessee. Riley says he tried to convey how important their contributions to the UK basketball program will be.

RILEY: "It's really about being significant. To be able to be part of the team 25-years ago that people still remember, you know, fondly and warmly, and to be able to come back and be honored and to sort of pass that on to this group of kids. Kentucky's really about significance, it's about tradition, it's about a story, and you're going to be part of that story forever. And if you ever do something significant, like we did, and if this team could ever do something significant, then they'll know that what they did here is what counted. I think that's what it's all about."

LEDFORD: Riley and Pitino aren't exactly strangers. The two squared off several times on the NBA hardwood. Riley describes the unique style that Pitino brought into professional basketball.

RILEY: "He brought in a philosophy that a lot of people really looked down on. They didn't think it was going to work. But you know, when you coach, you have to coach what you believe in. That's his philosophy. He doesn't care where it is, what level that he's going to play at, he's going to use that philosophy, and he pressed as hard as anybody's ever pressed in the NBA. Nobody believed he could hold up with it and he held up with it. I mean, it was ugly in the beginning, real ugly, you know, 70-80 fouls a game, but he took that New York Knick team, turned it around and made them believers. So he's very unique."

LEDFORD: Every time the UK coaching job has come open, Riley's name is invariably at the top of everyone's list of possible candidates. Riley, though, says UK fans shouldn't hold their breath.

RILEY: "No, I'm not a college coach. The only thing I really know is professional basketball. That's what I'm suited for, I think. If I ever decided to get back into it, it would be at that level. Plus, I don't think you're ever going to see a day that they're ever going to let this guy (Pitino) get away."

LEDFORD: It wasn't long after my talk with Pat that he did decide to get back into coaching. And, ironically, he'll be taking over the team that Rick Pitino once headed...the New York Knicks. Pat Riley may never coach the Kentucky Wildcats, but he'll always remain a giant figure in UK's basketball history.

LITTLE LOUIE

(Louie Dampier was a sharp-shooting guard from Indianapolis who chose to play his college basketball at the University of Kentucky. He was the chief outside threat for Rupp's Runts. He is also one of the most popular Wildcats of all-time.)

LEDFORD: Louie Dampier possessed one of the best jump shots the University of Kentucky has ever seen. He had range, too, often launching his on-target missiles from deep outside. He still stands as the eighth-leading scorer in UK history, finishing his three varsity seasons in 1967 with 1,575 points. Surprisingly, however, for a player known as a great shooter, Louie hated the 30-minute shooting session at practice each day.

DAMPIER: "You worked at it. You had to run and get the rebounds, run to your spot and take another shot. And Coach Rupp always wanted you to shoot from where you would shoot in the game. So as much as I hated that, I have to attribute my success to that regimental shooting. In my later years, my junior and senior years, I thought, 'What am I going to do to get through this shooting practice?' So I started making a game of it. We never had managers keep track of our shots, but I started doing that just to see what percentage I shot. And every once in awhile, there were seconds ticking off the clock while you'd take a shot and I would pretend that it was the final moments of a game. Adolph made a statement once that, 'God gave Louie the ability to shoot, but I took the credit.' "

LEDFORD: After Louie graduated from Kentucky, he signed with the Kentucky Colonels of the ABA. He took his patented jump shot with him, a shot that was made for that league's three-point line. It served him well, too, for by the time the ABA disbanded, Louie was the all-time leading scorer. The ABA disbanded in the late '70s, but being the leading scorer is still an honor Louie is proud of.

DAMPIER: "Well, it's something I'm proud of, but the thing is, the lack of longevity for the ABA is why I am the overall leading scorer. I know the year that we disbanded, (Julius) Erving and (Dan) Issel were right behind me. And they were scoring machines, so the only reason that I am the leading scorer is that they didn't play as many years. But nonetheless, I'm proud of it, and it's something that will always be because there's not an ABA anymore."

LEDFORD: Would Louie have welcomed the three-point line when he was playing for UK? What do you think?

DAMPIER: "Would have loved it, unless it would have been a psychological problem...just that there was a line there and it made three points. All of our plays, almost all of the plays that Rupp had for the guards, were designed for a 20-foot jump shot. A 20- to 22-foot jump shot. So, yeah, that would have been to my advantage, and to the advantage of the other guards who came off the picks and shot that shot."

LEDFORD: If college basketball had used the three-point line back in Louie's days, UK may have a different all-time leading scorer now. And it very well might have been Little Louie Dampier.

GIANT TRAGEDY

(Bill Spivey was the first seven-footer to play at the University of Kentucky, and before he saw his career prematurely — and unjustly — cut short, he would lead the Wildcats to an NCAA championship. He would also leave Big Blue fans wondering what-if.)

LEDFORD: Bill Spivey was the dominant big man in college basketball during his time at Kentucky. He scored 1,213 points in two years, leading the Cats to a 57-7 record. In 1950-51, Spivey teamed with Cliff Hagan and Frank Ramsey to give Adolph Rupp his third NCAA title in four years. He was a force, yet when he first arrived at Kentucky from Georgia, he wasn't all that intimidating.

SPIVEY: "He (Rupp) spotted some sort of raw talent in me, because when I came up here, I only weighed about 170 pounds. They fattened me up...got me up to 220."

LEDFORD: The task of beefing Spivey up was left to assistant coach Harry Lancaster. Rupp was out of the country that summer, so every two or three weeks, Lancaster would send a wire to the Baron reporting on Spivey's progress. Finally, after receiving a wire informing him that Spivey's weight had reached 185 pounds, Rupp shot a wire back to Lancaster saying, "I know Spivey can eat, but can he play basketball?"

SPIVEY: "That's a true story. They had me going through the cafeteria with two trays of food. I was supposed to eat four orders of potatoes, no six orders of potatoes, and drink four quarts of milk a day. And I had tickets to the theater downtown, passes, but they wouldn't let me in unless I stopped at Owen Williams' drugstore and had a malted milk before I went over there."

LEDFORD: Spivey proved just how dominant he was when he had his famous head-to-head showdown with Kansas All-American Clyde Lovellette. It was no contest. Spivey crushed Lovellette in every way. What does Spivey remember most about that famous duel?

SPIVEY: "The way that Rupp prepared me for the game. I'd say probably six weeks before the game — he never admitted to doing this — but they put pictures and clippings of Clyde Lovellette on my locker every day. Clippings about how great he was. So by game time, I was ready to go out and tear him apart, you know?"

LEDFORD: After leading the Wildcats to the national title, Spivey sat out his senior season because of NCAA sanctions. That UK team went 29-3 without the big guy, leaving many UK fans to wonder what the Cats might have done had he been there. Another NCAA championship perhaps? Spivey has no doubts that the Cats would have repeated.

SPIVEY: "Not in my mind, not with the team we had. No way. We would have probably gone undefeated, and I know it sounds a little egotistical, but I think we would have won it again."

LEDFORD: Bill Spivey is arguably the best big man to ever play for UK. What isn't arguable is that he's the most tragic figure in all of UK sports. Although he was never found guilty of any wrongdoings, he was banned from playing in the NBA. That remains one of the great injustices in sports history. Spivey would no doubt have been just as dominant in the pros as he was when he played for the Wildcats.

OLD RELIABLE

(Shelby Linville was known as "Old Reliable" for the way he consistently came through in the clutch in the big games. He was a key member on the University of Kentucky's 1951 NCAA championship team and one of the school's toughest competitors ever.)

LEDFORD: The 1951 Wildcats are perhaps the school's most underrated and least-appreciated team. They didn't have a catchy, colorful nickname like "The Fabulous Five" or "The Fiddlin' Five." What that team did have was a roster of great players, standout performers like Bill Spivey, Cliff Hagan, Frank Ramsey, Bobby Watson and Shelby Linville. Those Wildcats carved out a 32-2 record, including one stretch where they won 21 straight games. Despite that dominance, Linville says the NCAA tournament was anything but easy.

LINVILLE: "We had four games. It was kind of a mixed-up tournament in a sense, because they had our first game at Louisville. I remember we beat Louisville by 11 points. Then we went on up to Madison Square Garden and beat St. John's by about 16 points. Then we had that game with Illinois that went down to the last seconds before we won it. And then we had to fly out to Minneapolis to play the finals against Kansas State. I think we beat them by 10."

LEDFORD: There were some scary moments during that run for the title. In three of the four games, the Wildcats trailed at intermission. But every challenge was answered by Wildcat heroics. Linville had 23 points in the win over Louisville. Ramsey, Watson and Spivey keyed the win over St. John's. The Cats then faced Illinois in the semifinals, and with Spivey, Hagan and Skippy Whitaker on the bench with five fouls, Linville showed why he was known as "Old Reliable."

LINVILLE: "Well, I guess I was fortunate to score a lot of clutch goals at the end of the game, or the go-ahead goal, or whatever it might have been. Just lucky, I guess."

LEDFORD: Linville is being far too modest. Against Illinois, he scored 14 points, including the game-winning bucket with 12 seconds remaining. The Cats claimed the crown by beating Kansas State in their next outing. Linville says talent was one reason for that club's success. The presence of Rupp was another.

LINVILLE: "At that time, I think Coach Rupp was well advanced in the philosophy of the game. In later years, as he got older, I think it caught up with him. That's the reason there is so much parity with other teams. There are more players, bigger gyms, more draw for the other teams to kind of even things out. But even at that, I think the record of Kentucky has still been fabulous."

LEDFORD: Shelby Linville is still doing good deeds these days as a pastor in Middletown, Ohio. But in the Bluegrass State, he'll always be remembered as "Old Reliable"...the man who got the job done when it counted.

RUPP'S BARNYARD FIDDLERS

(The 1958 UK basketball team was known as The Fiddlin' Five. The starters were Vernon Hatton, Adrian Smith, Ed Beck, Johnny Cox and John Crigler. All that team did was fiddle around and win Kentucky's fourth NCAA trophy. Hatton, a senior guard that season, was the team's leading scorer.)

LEDFORD: Adolph Rupp was one of the most entertaining coaches of his time. His explanation of how teams played, though serious, always drew a few laughs. In 1958, he took four seniors and one junior and said they weren't concert pianists, they were just fiddlin' around. They became known as the Fiddlin' Five. Vernon Hatton recalls how the name came about.

HATTON: "They didn't have a name for us. They had The Fabulous Five, you know, and all these big names for the other teams, so they had to come up with a name for us. Coach Rupp, at the halftime and after the game, would say, 'You boys just fiddled around tonight.' He'd say you just almost won, almost didn't win, you know, and we'd usually win by a point or two. So really that's how it actually started, fiddlin' around, just like the name says."

LEDFORD: It was never more true than in the third game of the year against Temple. The game lasted three overtimes and was one of the most exciting college games ever played. Guard Adrian Smith missed a long shot at the end of regulation to send the game into overtime. Near the end of the first OT, the Cats were down two with one second left. Hatton remembers how they called his name for the last shot.

HATTON: "Adrian (Odie) Smith had already shot one just about the same length with one second left in the first overtime — it was a three overtime game — and he missed it by about 20 feet. And they wanted him to do it again. Coach Rupp said, 'Odie, you can do it this time.' And Coach (Harry) Lancaster stepped up and said, 'Coach Rupp, let's let Hatton take this shot.' So I got to thinking about it and I said, 'Yeah, Coach, let me take it, let me take it!' You know, I'd convinced myself I could make it. And then when I shot it, I watched it go up and I was praying and screaming and hollering. It went through, and it was the greatest shot I ever made."

LEDFORD: The Cats went on to score an 85-83 win. However, by season's end, Kentucky had six losses. That wasn't good news as NCAA tournament time rolled around. No team had ever won the NCAA title with six losses.

HATTON: "The six losses were a little deceiving in that one or two, maybe three of them were just one or two points. Close games, you know, Fiddlin' Five-type games. So we really did not ever doubt ourselves, that we could win the tournament. We were surprised when we did, but I have to give a lot of credit to having the Final Four at Louisville, where we had a packed house of all-Kentucky fans. That led us on, and we loved it."

LEDFORD: Once in Louisville, the Cats faced Temple again. This time, Hatton hit a shot at the buzzer to win the game. The victory put the Cats in the finals against Seattle, led by the great Elgin Baylor. Kentucky won that one as well, 84-72, giving Adolph Rupp his fourth and final NCAA championship. These days, Vernon Hatton is still living in Lexington, where he's an auctioneer and realtor. But it's as one of UK's truly great clutch players that Hatton is best remembered. And for helping turn a bunch of fiddlers into concert violinists.

MR. OUTSIDE

(If there's one constant thread that runs through the University of Kentucky's glorious basketball tradition, it's great shooters. Over the years, the Cats have had a long line of players who could fill it up. And few could light up a scoreboard faster than Larry Pursiful.)

LEDFORD: Larry Pursiful was recruited out of Four Mile, Ky., by Harry Lancaster. He became a starter during the 1960-61 season, but it was the next year that Pursiful really blossomed. Teaming with sophomore Cotton Nash, Pursiful helped lead the Cats to a 23-3 record and a share of the SEC crown. It was a season of surprising accomplishments, much like the season this year's UK team enjoyed.

PURSIFUL: "Well, it was very much like this year's team. We had lost about three or four starters from the previous year, so no one expected us to do anything. Cotton, of course, came in as a heralded sophomore, and, really, what happened was he got going inside and really carried the load. Then, of course, that got everybody watching him, which left me open outside. It really just was a good combination. (Carroll) Burchett and (Allen) Feldhaus and (Scotty) Baesler kind of added their dimension. Scotty, of course, was a defensive player and set the plays up. It just really worked out well. We got a good chemistry going, and like this year's team did, we just had a great year."

LEDFORD: The Pursiful-Nash duo was one of UK's most dynamic and successful. If the defense sagged on Nash, Pursiful made them pay by drilling the outside jumper. If they came out to get Pursiful, Nash worked his magic close to the bucket.

PURSIFUL: "Cotton was a terrific ballplayer. He was super...we made a good combination. Cotton worked inside and I worked outside. It was a treat to play with him."

LEDFORD: For Pursiful, the 20- to 25-foot jumper was almost like a layup. He was death from the perimeter. Given that, the obvious question is: How would he have liked the three-point shot?

PURSIFUL: "Well, the obvious answer is, I would have loved it. I still play, kick around a little bit, and I just look forward to playing on it. I would have loved the three-point shot."

LEDFORD: At 6-1, Pursiful wasn't the biggest or strongest player to ever wear the blue and white. What he was, though, was a tremendous competitor, a trait that Adolph Rupp looked for in all of his players.

PURSIFUL: "I enjoyed competing, enjoyed winning. You know, Coach Rupp kind of instilled that in you. He wanted you to win and play hard and that kind of carries over throughout your life."

LEDFORD: Larry Pursiful is currently the minister of activities at a small church in Louisville. He still plays quite a bit of basketball, and it wouldn't surprise me if he can out-shoot most of the youngsters he works with. That shouldn't bother them at all. Larry Pursiful could out-shoot just about everybody.

CHARISMATIC COTTON

(Cotton Nash was one of the greatest players to ever play at the University of Kentucky. Also, one of the most charismatic. He was a three-time All-American who reached the 1,000-point club at UK faster than any Wildcat before or since.)

LEDFORD: Cotton Nash burst on the scene as a sophomore during the 1961-62 season. The Cats weren't expected to do much that year, but with Nash leading the way, they finished with a 23-3 record and a share of the SEC title. If Nash played today, he'd be a big guard. In those days, though only 6-5, he played in the pivot. That he succeeded there is a tribute to his talent and courage. But Nash wasn't just a low-post player. He had great versatility, and that's what enabled him to succeed against bigger opponents.

NASH: "I guess, looking back on it, you can probably say I was an all-around player in the respect that I was probably not exceptional at any phase of the game, yet I was better than average or good at all of them. In today's game, I guess I would be described as a finesse-type player. I was one step quicker than most of the opponents, even though I gave up a lot of height playing center for three years. That is what got me by, my quickness."

LEDFORD: Since Nash was something of a free spirit and a player who needed some latitude on the court, it would figure that he'd have trouble playing for a stern disciplinarian like Baron Adolph Rupp. In fact, legend has it that the two didn't get along. Not so, says Nash.

NASH: "I really enjoyed playing his style of ball. It was a no-nonsense business when we were out on the court with him. We were out there an hour and 45 minutes a day. We got there on time...nobody was allowed to be late. He was very, very efficient. I appreciated that fact. I guess that was just my personality; it lends itself a little in that direction."

LEDFORD: It was during Nash's time at UK that the Wildcats reached the No. 1 ranking in the polls for the first time in over six years. That came after what Nash calls his most memorable win as a Wildcat.

NASH: "That game would have to be the finals of the Sugar Bowl Tournament in New Orleans my senior year. We beat Duke, who at the time, was ranked No. 1. They had two seven-footers and a 6-8 guy on the front line. We came out that night and matched up 6-5, 6-3 and 6-3 on the front line with them. We beat them by two points. About three or four days later we were accorded the No. 1 ranking in the country."

LEDFORD: Nash was one of the most recognizable players ever to play at UK. Even now, more than 25 years later, that remains unchanged.

NASH: "As the years go on, it gradually diminishes, which is good and bad, I guess. It's bad for your ego when nobody recognizes you anymore (laughs). And I guess I still appreciate it when a person comes up to me and says, 'Hello, I remember this, I remember that.' "

LEDFORD: In the vast galaxy of UK stars, few have shone brighter than Cotton Nash. He was, in every sense of the word, a superstar.

MR. CLUTCH

(Mike Casey came to Kentucky as the premier player in a recruiting class that also included Dan Issel and Mike Pratt. While he was at UK, Casey established himself as a player who did what it took to win.)

LEDFORD: Mike Casey was like most Kentucky kids growing up...he dreamed of someday donning a Wildcat uniform and going to war for Adolph Rupp. Unlike most of those would-be Wildcats, Casey had the talent to see his dream come true. He decided before his senior season at Shelby County High School that he would attend UK, but that didn't keep the coaching wolves off his doorstep.

CASEY: "I had committed to UK the fall of my senior year, then asked that Coach Rupp and Coach (Harry) Lancaster just leave me alone and let me go ahead and concentrate on my senior year. About halfway through my senior year, U of L came into the picture. And then at the very last, UCLA Coach (John) Wooden made two or three calls and really tried to persuade me to come out there. But my heart was set."

LEDFORD: The Casey-Issel-Pratt trio represented one of the finest recruiting hauls in UK history. Issel would go on to become UK's all-time leading scorer, Casey would finish ninth and Pratt 19th on that prestigious list. Combined, they would score more than 5,000 points.

CASEY: "It was a joy to play with those two guys because they played the type of ball that Coach Rupp wanted...fast-break, get the ball to the open man. Of course, we always got accused of not having enough basketballs to go around out there. But we all got our shots somehow."

LEDFORD: Prior to his final season at UK, Casey was involved in an automobile accident that forced him to sit out a year. That UK team just missed a trip to the Final Four. UK fans have always felt that had Casey been playing, the Cats would have been there. So does Casey.

CASEY: "I think we would have gotten there. There were a couple of games, like the Jacksonville game when Dan fouled out after they called two charging calls in the last four minutes that were really questionable calls, where there was nobody there to pick up the slack in scoring. I like to think that I could have done that in case Dan fouled out."

LEDFORD: If I were picking my all-clutch team, Mike Casey's name would be at or near the top. He wanted the ball when it counted and he seldom failed to come through with the big bucket when it was needed the most. Mike Casey was one of UK's greats.

BIG DAN

(It's been more than 20 years since Dan Issel wore the Kentucky blue and white, but he is still the most prolific point-maker in UK's storied basketball history.)

LEDFORD: Nineteen sixty-seven was the worst season of Adolph Rupp's 41 years of coaching the Kentucky Wildcats. The team won 13 and lost 13. About the only thing that made the season palatable was the undefeated freshman team. The nucleus of the team was Dan Issel, Mike Casey and Mike Pratt. All three went on to start as sophomores, and with Casey leading the scoring, the Cats went 22-5. The next season Issel took over the scoring load as UK was 23-5. Many fans dreamed of another NCAA title for the Cats the following season, but a bad accident broke up the Issel-Casey-Pratt trio.

ISSEL: "Mike Pratt and Larry Steele were the forwards. If you remember, Mike Casey had just had that terrible automobile accident and fractured his leg, so he wasn't able to play. Most of that year, we started Terry Mills and Jim Dinwiddie in the backcourt. Stan Key started occasionally as well, but, that was, for most of my senior year, the starting five."

LEDFORD: The injury to Mike Casey set the team back, but with Dan Issel leading the way, the Cats won 26 times and lost only twice. Issel had many great performances, yet oddly enough, it was a blowout that turned out to be Big Dan's favorite game.

ISSEL: "Well, Cawood, since we never won a championship while I was at Kentucky, I think the best one was probably my senior year at Ole Miss when I was fortunate enough to set the single-game record and break Cotton Nash's career scoring record all in the same night."

LEDFORD: Issel was having one of those nights that shooters dream about. He was hot from the field and the free throw line.

ISSEL: "I obviously was having a pretty hot night, so when Coach Rupp took me out, one of the trainers, Doug Phillips, told him that I was only, I think, six points away from breaking Cliff Hagan's 51-points mark. Coach Rupp put me back in and I was able to get 53. As soon as I scored that last basket, he took me out of the game."

LEDFORD: Issel's 53 points is still the UK record for one game. And had Rupp so chosen, the big guy could have scored even more.

ISSEL: "Well, I think there was still a couple of minutes to go in the game, but breaking it by two and getting that record was a big, big thrill for me."

LEDFORD: There was another reason why breaking that record was such a thrill for Dan. He did it while someone special was looking on.

ISSEL: "My father used to go on one road trip a year with the team. Of course, he saw every game I played in Memorial Coliseum, but he went on that road trip that year to Ole Miss and Mississippi State. He was kind of my good luck charm. I always played real well when my dad was in the stands. Probably, he was more thrilled about the record than I was."

LEDFORD: When the 1970 season was over, Dan Issel had scored 2,138 career points, the most ever by a Wildcat. His 53 points against Ole Miss is also a UK record, and while Dan was known more for being a scorer, his 1,078 rebounds is a school record as well. With those numbers backing him up, it's hard to argue against Dan Issel being the Kentucky Wildcats' greatest player.

A SUPER KITTEN

(He was a crowd favorite during his Wildcat years of 1973-75. His first collegiate contest ushered in the Joe B. Hall era at Kentucky. His last collegiate game was also the last game John Wooden coached. He led Anderson County High to the finals of the state tournament. Can you name this Wildcat?)

LEDFORD: If you guessed Jimmy Dan Connor you were correct. Jimmy Dan came from Lawrenceburg, Ky., just 25 minutes west of Lexington. As a freshman in 1972, he teamed with Kevin Grevey, Mike Flynn and several others to become the Super Kittens, the freshman team that never lost. Connor remembers his UK career well.

CONNOR: "We won like the last 14 games in a row to win the conference my sophomore year, and, you know, those things are kind of fun. We had the fun and the bad. We also had a 13-13 year, which was not fun. But the great thing about playing at Kentucky is that the fans are so knowledgeable about the game, it's good and bad. You go 13-13, they don't like it, but that's good. They demand that you do better."

LEDFORD: Connor's last game was his most memorable. It was the NCAA championship game in 1975. Kentucky had beaten Marquette, Central Michigan, Indiana and Syracuse to reach the championship game. Only one team stood between UK and a fifth NCAA title...the UCLA Bruins. The Cats lost 92-85 in John Wooden's last game as coach.

CONNOR: "You go up against a legend and then the night before the game, he announces his retirement. There are two things I would have liked to have had happen. I would have liked to have played them east of the Mississippi, and I would have liked to play them when he wasn't announcing his retirement. That made it awfully hard for us. It was almost like, well, I didn't want to beat him because it was his last game. Of course, that's not true, but it added a lot of pressure on the game and gave them a boost that I think they needed. I think we had a better team than they did."

LEDFORD: To Jimmy Dan, the UCLA defeat did not cloud the Cats' accomplishments.

CONNOR: "Getting into the Final Four is really what you want to do. After that, obviously you want to win the national championship, there's no question about it. The worst thing that happened to us was beating Indiana in the finals of the Mideast regional. They were undefeated at the time, so that was almost like winning the NCAA for us. But obviously we went out there and we wanted to bring another one back to Kentucky to carry on the great tradition that's been going on here for a lot of years. We just came up a little short."

LEDFORD: Jimmy Dan Connor averaged 12 points a game each of his three seasons at UK. Nowadays, he's in the insurance business in Louisville. He still attends UK games and, don't tell anyone, even a few U of L games too. I guess basketball still runs thick in his blood.

COOL KYLE

(Kyle Macy played but three years at the University of Kentucky, yet established himself as one of the most idolized players to ever slip on a UK jersey.)

LEDFORD: Kyle Macy was the classic Kentucky player...clean-cut, soft spoken and owner of a pure jump shot. Macy, however, didn't originally sign with UK. He signed with Purdue, then transferred to UK after one season with the Boilermakers. It was, he says, a move that needed to be made.

MACY: "I just wasn't happy at Purdue. I mean, the school was great and I had a lot of friends there. I enjoyed the one year I spent there, other than just the basketball. I was highly recruited by them and felt like I was going to get an opportunity to play, which I probably never would have had if Bruce Parkinson, whose father played here at UK, hadn't gone down with a wrist injury. He had a broken wrist, so after the fourth game of the year, I moved in to a starting spot and scored 24 the first game and 38 in our first Big Ten game. But then, from then on, it seemed like I was seeing the ball less and less and nothing was ever said. Nothing ever happened to make me believe that things were ever going to change back to the way I thought they should."

LEDFORD: Travis Ford transferred from Missouri to Kentucky last season and, like Macy, has had to sit and watch for a year as a redshirt. Kyle says that year on the sidelines sometimes feels like more than a year.

MACY: "It's tough. I mean, there are days when you feel like you're doing OK. You do get to practice, which is a good thing, whereas a Prop 48 player doesn't get to practice. So in that instance, it's good. You still feel sometimes like you're a part of the team. Then there are other days where it's really a struggle. You kind of feel like, you know, I'm just sitting here not doing anything, wasting time. It's a long year. But I tell you, when it's finally over, and Travis probably just went through this, when the last game is over, it's a great relief. I was real sad when the team lost in the East regionals, but I was also real happy because I knew from that point on, I was eligible and that I was finally going to get a chance to play."

LEDFORD: When Kyle finally did get to play, he left his mark in many ways...a national championship, SEC Player of the Year, game-winning shots and deadly accuracy at the charity stripe are just a few of his great accomplishments. It was a ritual Macy performed at the free throw line that became his trademark — reaching down and grabbing his socks before shooting each shot.

MACY: "I don't really know when that started. It wasn't a conscious effort on my part to say, 'OK, I'm going to do this.' I think it was just from practice and finding out as you play a game that your whole body's full of sweat and your uniform is wet. If you wear two pairs of socks, your outside pair is usually not wet. That's the only part of the uniform that's dry when you want to wipe your hands off. So it's not like it started in the sixth grade and I've been doing it ever since. It just developed over the years."

LEDFORD: Did Kyle consider it to be a superstition?

MACY: "No, not a superstition. It's just part of the routine that I developed. You know, you're shooting free throws and you want to have a set routine to help you concentrate. It helps you relax, and it helps you shoot a better percentage at the free throw line."

LEDFORD: After a successful pro career that ended last year in Europe, Macy is now dabbling in broadcasting. But he doesn't rule out getting into the coaching profession. That would be fitting. After all, Kyle was always thought of as a coach on the floor.

Considered an "on the floor" coach, Kyle Macy led the Wildcats to the 1978 national championship with his heady play.

UNSUNG HERO

(Thirteen years ago, the University of Kentucky Wildcats were sitting on top of the college basketball world. Coach Joe B. Hall's club capped off a magnificent 30-2 season by defeating Duke 94-88 to capture the school's fifth NCAA championship. One of the unsung heroes on that UK team was Truman Claytor.)

LEDFORD: That 1978 UK team was loaded. Rick Robey and Mike Phillips patrolled the paint area with authority. Jack Givens was deadly from the perimeter. Truman Claytor and Kyle Macy were a solid backcourt duo. James Lee and Jay Shidler provided rebounding and scoring punch off the bench. It was an experienced team with no glaring weaknesses. Because of those ingredients, it was also a team that was expected to win. Despite all that experience, Claytor says the season didn't get off to a ringing start...expecially for him and Macy.

CLAYTOR: "That first game that we were playing, Kyle Macy and myself were at guard and we were supposed to come out and run a certain play. Well, we both forgot the play. We were so excited we couldn't get our mouths open to call the play. I just looked at Kyle, he looked at me, and finally it just came out after about five minutes."

LEDFORD: The '78 Cats roared from the gate, winning their first 14 games before losing. That quick start wasn't surprising. Claytor says he and his teammates had begun thinking about winning the national title a long time before the first jump shot was taken.

CLAYTOR: "We dedicated ourselves over the summer. We all stayed here in Lexington that summer, and we made up our mind that was our goal. We made a commitment to win the NCAA championship the following year."

LEDFORD: During the past 13 years, the game of basketball has changed somewhat. Today's game seems to be dominated more by outstanding individual play rather than by teamwork and togetherness. Claytor, though, says it doesn't matter. As far as he's concerned, that '78 UK team could hold its own today.

CLAYTOR: "I think we could play with the teams of today because we could do a lot of things really good. We could run the fastbreak, or slow it down and run the inside game. We played excellent defense and, most of all, we played together as a team. Each player on that team knew his role. In order to have a good championship team, you have to have that right chemistry."

LEDFORD: During that Final Four weekend in St. Louis, the Wildcat players were portrayed as grim and serious while the players from Duke, Arkansas and Notre Dame were having all the fun. Claytor, however, says that he and his fellow Wildcats have had all the fun since.

CLAYTOR: "I've had a great time since that happened. We made a commitment to win it, we were there in St. Louis to accomplish something, and we've had all our fun after we won the championship."

LEDFORD: Claytor has continued his successful ways. He lives in his native Toledo, Ohio, where he works as an alcohol and drug treatment counselor. But it's in the Bluegrass State that T.C. will always be remembered for playing a vital role on one of UK's finest teams. Truman Claytor...an unsung Wildcat hero.

SHOT OF DREAMS

(Every high school basketball player dreams of playing in the Sweet 16. And every player dreams of making a last-second shot to give his team the state championship. Paul Andrews did just that.)

LEDFORD: Back in 1982, Laurel County High School came away with the most coveted title in all of Kentucky High School sports — the Sweet 16 trophy for winning the Kentucky High School Basketball Championship. Paul Andrews was a junior guard for the Cardinals. They were a top five team in the state almost the entire season, finishing with a 33-3 record. But it was during the 36th game — in the final ticks of the clock — that glory struck for Andrews and his teammates.

ANDREWS: "We topped it off with winning the state championship, which we really, really wanted. The year before we were really disappointed because we made it to the state tournament but really didn't do anything. We were beaten the first round. So we wanted to go back the next year and try to redeem ourselves and do a little bit better."

LEDFORD: They did a lot better, thanks to Paul. North Hardin had advanced to the finals and looked to be unbeatable. Brett Burrow and Robbie Valentine were the chief guns from North Hardin. Laurel County was outmanned and outsized, and to top it off, the players were worn out.

ANDREWS: "I was really, really tired...the whole team was tired. I just felt the game was going to go into overtime, and I kept telling everybody that I just didn't want the game to go into overtime, so that's why I hit the shot. But really it was just something that happened. I intercepted a pass and my instincts took over. I just took three dribbles and let it go, and was lucky enough that it went in."

LEDFORD: With those few ticks left, Brett Burrow's errant pass had found a temporary home...in the hands of Andrews. As the buzzer sounded, Paul's shot nestled through the twine, giving the Cardinals a 53-51 win and the state title. Truthfully now, Paul, did you think the shot was going in when it left your hands?

ANDREWS: "No, I really didn't think it was going in. I thought that it had a chance, but it really didn't hit me until it went through the basket. Then I was really just stunned. I was immobilized. I just laid there on the floor and all my teammates just came and jumped on me. It was something that really happened and I'm just glad it happened to me."

LEDFORD: Paul Andrews earned second-team all-state honors that season. He made first-team the next year. After committing to Tennessee his senior year, he changed his mind and signed with the Cats. But after four years at Laurel County and four years at Kentucky, Paul's shining moment in the spotlight came 40 feet from the basket in the 1982 Sweet 16. It will live forever as the shot heard 'round the state.

REX

(Rex Chapman came to the University of Kentucky as something of a phenomenon, and at the time he decided to turn pro he was arguably the most popular and most recognizable person in this state. Currently, Rex is in the NBA with the Charlotte Hornets.)

LEDFORD: Rex Chapman hit UK like a meteorite. Few athletes have ever arrived on the Wildcat campus with such force. His light shone brilliantly from the beginning, and it was at its brightest when he chose to go pro. As for his days at UK, Rex says he remembers them with great fondness.

CHAPMAN: "My two years at UK were fun. I had a great deal of fun. They were hard at times for a guy just coming out of high school. I really felt like I spent about three years at Kentucky. My senior year in high school I signed early, so I think the fans felt I was a part of the organization already, a part of the program already."

LEDFORD: Like most newcomers to the pro ranks, Rex struggled with his game. But even then, everyone knew it was just a matter of time before he would find his niche, which he did. But according to Rex, the game isn't the difficult part. It's the off-court adjustments that present the biggest challenges.

CHAPMAN: "Just being out on your own in a city where you don't know many people is a tough task to take on. I think that's the biggest thing. Off-the-court adjustment is, I think, far greater than on the court. You can pick up basketball if you know how to play and you have talent. You're going to pick up the basketball part. The hard part is getting the sleep, getting the right food and doing what you have to do to play night in and night out."

LEDFORD: Rex Chapman's basketball career has been filled with success. Still, though, there is one nagging failure that haunts him...not making the 1988 Olympic team. With the pros now eligible for the 1992 Olympics, Rex may get another shot at fulfilling that dream. Would he consider it?

CHAPMAN: "I would consider it, I think, from the standpoint that I haven't played in it before. Between now and 1992, in order for that to happen, I would have to improve my game dramatically. There are a lot of other great players who would be considered."

LEDFORD: Rex Chapman always wanted to play in the NBA. His dream of going head to head with the Michael Jordans and the Magic Johnsons has come true. And Rex says he hasn't been disappointed.

CHAPMAN: "As you grow older, it's everything and more. You know, you grow to realize that if you're fortunate enough to do it for awhile, then you can set yourself up in a financial situation where maybe you don't have to worry so much as soon as you finish playing."

LEDFORD: Rex Chapman is one of the most exciting basketball players I've ever seen. He could do it all, and he did it with flair. His stay at UK may have been brief, but it was long enough to leave a lasting impression on those who saw him play.

One of the most popular players ever to don the UK blue and white, Rex Chapman now toils in the National Basketball Association for the Charlotte Hornets.

MOUNTAIN HERO

(Playing for the Kentucky Wildcats can be tough. The demands are unrealistic and the exposure can be suffocating. There's a period of adjustment for every high school player who signs with the Wildcats. It's even tougher when the player comes from the mountains of Eastern Kentucky to live in the big city of Lexington for the first time. Few know more about that burden than Richie Farmer.)

LEDFORD: Richie Farmer saw his dreams become reality in 1988 when he signed to play basketball at Kentucky. The small sharp shooter from Manchester led his Clay County basketball team to five consecutive state tournaments. Farmer then topped off his storybook career by signing to wear the blue and white at UK.

FARMER: "I think it has to be the greatest thing in the world. I think most of the people in the mountains are the greatest basketball fans in the world, especially University of Kentucky fans. As a kid, I always grew up dreaming of playing for UK someday, and now that it's happened, it's just a dream come true."

LEDFORD: Richie has had his ups and downs at UK. The adjustment has been tough at times. But last year, he finally settled into a groove and began to show the basketball brilliance that made him a star in high school. Not every Eastern Kentucky native has done well at UK. Some have even departed early. Farmer says it's a situation that affects each person in a different way.

FARMER: "I think it's different for different individuals. I know where I grew up, it's a real small town, everybody knows everybody in the whole town. When you come here, I

Richie Farmer, former Clay County High School star, considers playing at the University of Kentucky a childhood dream come true.

think just the pace of life is a little bit faster. It takes a lot of adjustment mentally and physically, you know, on the basketball court as well as in the classroom. It's just a big adjustment."

LEDFORD: Basketball players also have the extra burden that goes along with representing their hometown. When Richie finally signed with the Cats, he could have won a race for mayor of Manchester. He was the town's pride and joy. While it seems to be an enviable position, there's quite a bit of pressure that goes along with fame.

FARMER: "A lot of people back in Clay County, they like to see me play well and do good. Anytime you can do that, they think it looks good on the whole community where you're from. And I guess it does. But you can't really look at it as pressure to come up here and play well for all them. It's something that you want to do in your heart. It's something they appreciate and love, but when I don't play well, they really don't get on me that much. They know that I'm trying my best."

LEDFORD: Since Richie has been through the pressure cooker, what advice does he have for the youngsters who would like to follow in his footsteps?

FARMER: "You have to work hard every day and try to improve on your individual game, as well as the team game. Just play hard. If you've got the dedication and the drive to do it, then maybe someday it can happen."

LEDFORD: Richie Farmer. Hometown hero. Mountain hero. UK hero. A good ol' boy with a mountain twang as sharp as his jump shot.

ALL IN THE FAMILY

(John Pelphrey may look like Opie Taylor on The Andy Griffith Show, but his importance to the UK basketball team in 1990-91 can't be overstated. In that regards, he resembled Larry Bird — the glue that kept the Cats together.)

LEDFORD: You can call it the Pelphrey way of life. Before Jack and Jenny Pelphrey began their family, they planned on their sons and daughters participating in sports at the highest level. That's exactly what has happened. Oldest son John is the star on the UK basketball team. John's younger brother Jerry is a reserve for nationally-ranked East Tennessee State. So I asked John if his parents forced them into sports or were they just guided in that general direction.

PELPHREY: "They didn't really push us into anything. It was always something where if we wanted to, we were able to. They were really kind of involved with the high school athletics and events that were going on there because they were both teachers and they took active parts in such roles as cheerleading and coaching. They were always around the games. It was something that we just kind of picked up because we had a love for it. My mom and dad were very knowledgeable about it, so it was really pretty easy to get hung up on athletics."

LEDFORD: Many times, sons and daughters are taken advantage of by their parents. All too often it's a situation where the parent is living out a dream by forcing it upon the child. The history of sports is filled with examples of athletes going astray because of the undue pressure put on them by their parents. Pelphrey says that wasn't the case in his family.

PELPHREY: "It's something that I always wanted to be in. We always thought it would be a great situation to be in, being highly recruited and end up playing in such a great environment as Kentucky basketball, knowing that so many people looked at it with great respect and pride. So it's a situation that I've really always wanted to be in, especially because we expect to do well in those kinds of situations. But the pressure has never really been there for us, because we've just wanted to succeed and be the best we possibly can."

LEDFORD: John's dedication to the sport has paid big dividends. Last season, he blossomed into an all-conference performer with his deadly three-point shooting, his timely passes and his spirited leadership. His contributions on the court won him an MVP trophy. However, the Paintsville native admits that he didn't know if his years of devotion to basketball would lead him to stardom when he signed with the Wildcats.

PELPHREY: "Well, I really didn't know because they did have a lot of great players coming in to join the players that were already here. I wasn't sure. I knew I was a year or two away, so I registered and even after that, it really didn't look too good because we had some great people like Shawn Kemp and Chris Mills and Eric Manuel. Then things really turned bad for us all as far as the program went. But it really turned out to be good for the guys who were here and stayed with the program and who got a chance to play. Playing for the University of Kentucky can be so much love. We're just happy that we've been lucky and have been able to do some good things."

LEDFORD: John Pelphrey has one more year to do some even better things, like get his Wildcats to the Final Four. Given his success story, don't be surprised if he does just that.

Swingman John Pelphrey's dedication to basketball has allowed him to raise his standard of play to an All-Southeastern Conference level.

SHOCKER

(The longest home-court winning streak in NCAA history belongs to the University of Kentucky. The Wildcats won 129-straight home games in a streak that began Jan. 4, 1943 and ended Jan. 8, 1955 when Georgia Tech scored a stunning 59-58 upset in Memorial Coliseum. Former UK assistant coach Lake Kelly was a member of that Georgia Tech team.)

LEDFORD: Georgia Tech was said to be the worst team on Kentucky's 1954-55 schedule, and the Yellow Jackets had done nothing to discredit that prediction. When they rolled into Lexington to face UK, the Yellow Jackets were fresh off of a loss to Sewanee. Kentucky, meanwhile, entered the Tech game undefeated with a 7-0 worksheet. Former UK assistant coach Lake Kelly, a Flemingsburg, Ky., native, remembers the game prior to Kentucky.

KELLY: "We went to Sewanee and we played horrible. And Sewanee beat us. I felt, 'Gosh, we're going into Kentucky, we're going to Lexington and we're going to get totally annihilated.' "

LEDFORD: Just a few weeks earlier, Kelly had returned home for the holidays and gone to the Coliseum to catch the Cats in action. While he was there, he took advantage of the situation by doing a little scouting for his team.

KELLY: "It just so happened that during the Christmas holidays I came home and went to a game at the Coliseum. I picked up a few things that I saw them do, and I took them back and we went over some of those things. And lo and behold, those things were very much a key."

LEDFORD: Kelly's notes on Kentucky's offensive and defensive schemes played a big role in Tech's victory. The game stayed close throughout and with 12 seconds left, Georgia Tech guard Joe Helms nailed a 12-footer to give the Yellow Jackets the lead at 59-58. Kentucky had one last chance, but a Linville Puckett jumper was short and the subsequent tips wouldn't go down. Georgia Tech had ended the Wildcats' consecutive string of home victories. The loss was a big shocker for the many Wildcat fans in attendance, many of whom had never seen a UK team lose.

KELLY: "When that buzzer went off, the 12,000 or so fans at the game just sat there. I mean absolutely sat there in total shock and dismay. Finally they began to get up slowly and leave the arena. It was a shock to them. I didn't know until afterwards that it was 129-straight games that they'd won at home. And I thought, 'My God, that record is something that probably will never be duplicated.' "

LEDFORD: That win put Georgia Tech on the map in college basketball. It also served as a preview of things to come for Lake Kelly, who would go on to become a distinguished basketball coach at the high school and collegiate levels. His coaching career and UK's record-breaking home winning streak came about because of a visit home during the Christmas holidays. Thanks to Lake Kelly's trip home, it turned out to be a happy holiday in Georgia and a gloomy holiday in Kentucky.

UNLIKELY WIN

(It may have been the most surprising comeback in Kentucky basketball history, a come-from-behind win over Kansas. The Cats had a host of heroes that night, and one of the biggest was All-American guard Kyle Macy.)

LEDFORD: It was Dec. 9, 1978 when Kansas came calling. Kentucky was trying to protect a 20-game home winning streak, but had lost four players from the previous championship season. Junior guard Kyle Macy was nursing a thigh injury, so he wasn't 100 percent. The game was a barnburner. Most Kentucky fans remember it vividly. Include Macy in that group.

MACY: "That was a game we really didn't have any reason winning. I mean, we were completely out of the game. It looked like it was over. We were down six or seven, whatever, with 30 seconds, I think. We got a few steals, fortunately. Dwight Anderson made a few nice plays. He made one steal, kicked the ball over to me and I got a basket. Then they ended up calling a timeout with no time left, or with like one second left, I guess, and they didn't have one, so a technical foul was called. Fortunately, I got the free throw to go in and that put us in the lead. It was unbelievable. That game was over, we had lost that game, but somehow pulled it out."

LEDFORD: Kentucky hadn't led since the score was 10-8 early in the game. Macy didn't even start the second half...his injured thigh had tightened up during the break. With the Cats behind, Macy re-entered. And with just under three minutes left in regulation, Kansas was up by two with the ball and in its patented four-corner offense. Time for Macy to make a big play. Here's how I saw the unlikely drama unfold.

LEDFORD CALL: "Guy comes out at long range, inside the last three minutes, Guy to Mokeski, back to Guy working the left side. He brings it back out to backcourt, swings it toward the top of the key...stolen by Macy...Macy running to the other end, lays it up and it's good!"

LEDFORD: That bucket by Macy knotted the score at 56 and sent the game into overtime. UK guard Jay Shidler had fouled out during regulation. Truman Claytor fouled out with 1:09 left in the extra frame, bringing freshman Dwight Anderson into the game. By this time, Kansas had taken control. With 31 seconds left the scoreboard read 66-60. It was over...or it should have been. Seven thousand fans had left the arena. But it wasn't finished. A bucket and two charity tosses by Anderson cut the lead to two and kept UK's chances alive. Barely. Ten seconds remained. Kansas' ball.

LEDFORD CALL: "In-bounds play and it's almost intercepted...it is intercepted. Kentucky's got it. Kyle Macy...good! It's 66-66 with three seconds to go...and Kansas has called a timeout."

LEDFORD: Two mistakes for Kansas. A bad pass that the hustling Anderson saved to Macy, and its sixth timeout. Teams are only allowed five. So not only did Macy tie it with his jumper, he would now step to the line to shoot one technical free throw. The crowd turned deathly silent. Ralph Hacker set the stage.

HACKER CALL: "One shot...Kyle Macy...Mr. Cool from Peru, Indiana,...got it, got it!"

LEDFORD: The Cats had come back to score a 67-66 victory. Everyone was shocked, including Macy, who said the Cats won because they refused to quit.

MACY: "You never give up as a player until the buzzer sounds. But at that point, you know, with about 40 seconds left in the game, it didn't look very encouraging. But we hung tough, and it just shows that it pays to play until the end."

LEDFORD: Kansas and Kentucky in 1978. What a game. And what a never-say-die comeback by the Wildcats.

Kentucky overcame the odds to post a 67-66 "never say die" victory against Kansas during the 1978 season.

HALL'S GUTTY CALL

(UK captured its last NCAA championship in 1978. That title didn't come easy, and it didn't come without an incredibly bold move by Coach Joe B. Hall against Florida State. It was not just a bold move by Hall; it was, many say, a move that could have cost him his job had it failed.)

LEDFORD: The first round of the Mideast regionals in 1978 matched No. 1 Kentucky against upstart Florida State in Knoxville. The Wildcats were heavy favorites to put the Seminoles aside with little trouble. UK was loaded that year, with a starting quintet that featured Rick Robey, Mike Phillips, Jack Givens, Truman Claytor and Kyle Macy. Despite the strength and experience of that lineup, the Cats came out flat and fell behind early. Here's how I called it as the Seminoles grabbed control.

LEDFORD CALL: "Jack Givens, going to the baseline with a jump shot on the move, won't go, grabbed by Anderson, and, boy, they've come out running it. They are running it, they still are moving. Here is a jump shot...good from the free throw line by Diller. He has 13 points and that's the biggest lead of the game. Florida State, 34-27. On top by seven points now. And Kentucky turns it over, steps called. Time out. Florida State right now is threatening to blow Kentucky out of it with 4:40 to go in the first half."

LEDFORD: That string of plays epitomized the entire first half for Kentucky. At halftime, the Cats found themselves down 39-32. Hall was fuming. His starters had been ineffective, so the angry Hall responded by making the gutsiest move of his coaching career. He inserted "shock troops" Dwane Casey, Lavon Williams and Fred Cowan to start the second half. Casey, the former UK assistant coach, remembers the moment well.

CASEY: "I remember Freddie Cowan looked over at me and said, 'Dwane, he has finally lost his mind. He's finally just flipped out.' You know, because Freddie couldn't believe that we were going to start the second half, but, you know, looking back, Coach Hall knew what he was doing and it was a great move, probably one of the gutsier moves of the 1978 season."

LEDFORD: The tone for the Cats was set as the youngsters crashed the boards and outhustled the Seminoles. Their energy and fullcourt scrappiness enabled the Cats to claw their way back into the thick of the battle. Finally, with just under 10 minutes to play, their effort paid off. Here's how I called it.

LEDFORD CALL: "Robey on the high post with Macy wide open...15-footer, got it! Kentucky has the lead for the first time since way back a long time ago, 54-53. Florida State wants a time out. Kentucky 54, Florida State 53 with 8:33 left in the game!"

LEDFORD: Cowan, Casey and Williams had teamed with regulars Macy and Phillips to help the Cats make their dramatic comeback charge. Their play also served as a wake-up call for the benched regulars, who returned with a fury to put the finishing touches on UK's 85-76 victory.

CASEY: "We went out and set the tempo for the game and, really, in essence, wore Florida State out. Then the first team came back in and finished them off. I think that set the tone for the rest of the NCAA tournament."

LEDFORD: Freddie Cowan and Dwane Casey weren't the only persons to think Hall had gone off the deep end. As the drama was being played out, the entire basketball community thought Hall was nuts. But in the end, it was Hall who had the last laugh. And his Wildcats had their national championship.

Orchestrating the march to the 1978 NCAA championship, Wildcat coach Joe B. Hall proved to be a master tactition when he inserted his "shock troops" in the Wildcats' 85-76 opening-round win against Florida State.

MASTER POINT

(Jim Master was the classic shooting guard, one of the purest jump shooters in UK history. However, on one critical occasion, Master moved to the point guard position and ad-libbed a play that lifted the Wildcats to a two-point win over Auburn in the SEC tournament title game.)

LEDFORD: Kentucky versus Auburn has always been a cat fight, but never was it more so than on March 10, 1984. It was the title game of the SEC tournament. Auburn had the "Round Mound of Rebound," Charles Barkley, and the equally-talented Chuck Person. Kentucky was loaded, led by Twin Towers Sam Bowie and Melvin Turpin. The game was a nail-biter from the opening tipoff. The lead changed often, and no team led by more than four points the entire time. With the score tied 49-49, Jim Master hit Kenny Walker with the deciding bucket as time expired. Jim recalls the play.

MASTER: "Dicky Beal was our point guard that year and I was the second guard, the two-guard. The play was designed to go to him out of bounds, and then he would do the dribbling off the pick and then feed it inside to Kenny Walker. Well, Auburn defensed the play very well. It was a tie game at the time, and we couldn't get it in-bounds to Dicky, so they threw it to me. For some reason I remembered what the play was. Sometimes I felt when I was out of it, I would, you know, wouldn't know how to run it from the point position. This time I did. I just went through with the play and dribbled down off the pick. Walker swung around, I got him the bounce pass inside, and the rest is history."

LEDFORD: Here's how you may have heard me call it in those final 14 seconds.

One of UK's purest shooters ever, Jim Master proved a point in the Cats' 51-49 1984 SEC title win against Auburn.

LEDFORD CALL: "It comes in to Master. They do not come in real tight on Master, and they're really shadowing Dicky Beal...they are really just guarding him without the ball. Jim Master gives it to Kenny Walker...Walker makes his move, goes up for a jump shot...it's good! And the horn sounds as it goes through, and it's Kenny Walker's turn to be the hero."

LEDFORD: UK was fortunate that Jim remembered what the point guard was supposed to do, because he wasn't known for his playmaking ability. It was shooting the "J" that made him famous.

MASTER: "I was just tickled to death that I remembered to do what the point guard was supposed to do. I think all of us were kind of surprised. But we won the game and that was a big stamp on our season. We'd won the SEC regular-season title, and then we became the first team ever, I believe, to win both the SEC title and the tournament title."

LEDFORD: Actually, it was the first time a team had won both the regular-season title and the tournament title in the same year since the tournament was renewed in 1979. Auburn coach Sonny Smith said it was the greatest game he'd ever been a part of. And his team didn't even win. Charles Barkley lay crying in the middle of the floor. The Auburn crowd was stunned. Master finished with just two assists for the game. Luckily, one came when the Wildcats needed it most.

MASTER: "I was not a great assist man in college. I generally liked to shoot the basketball, so it was fun to go through a play like that and to execute it like we were supposed to. It was a lot of fun. We got the basket and, of course, the victory."

LEDFORD: The 51-49 victory was just one more step in the Cats' run to the Final Four that season. The Wildcats finished 29-5 after losing to Georgetown in the semifinal round of the NCAA. But it was the cat fight with Auburn that still stands as one of the most memorable moments of that season, a moment that went UK's way because of Jim Master's ability to improvise during a crisis time.

UNRIVALED VICTORY

(The Kentucky-Tennessee football rivalry was once a great matchup between the neighboring states. It was, and still is, the battle for the beer barrel. One of the great victories for the Wildcats came in Knoxville back in 1954. The hero for UK that day was All-American end Howard Schnellenberger.)

LEDFORD: Whenever the Cats and Volunteers square off on the gridiron, you can expect a fierce battle for the full 60 minutes. On Nov. 20, 1954, it was no different. The Wildcats traveled to Knoxville that Saturday, where they hadn't won in 30 years. The Vols were riding a 4-4 record while the Cats were 6-3. Current Louisville head coach Howard Schnellenberger was a left end on that UK team. He remembers the day well.

SCHNELLENBERGER: "We had a knockdown traditional Kentucky-Tennessee game. The weather was terrible. It had been raining and the field was muddy."

LEDFORD: It may have been cold and wet in Knoxville, but the action was hot on the field. Kentucky was down 13-7 after blocking Tennessee's extra point in the third quarter. With three-and-a-half minutes remaining in the game, quarterback Bob Hardy had driven the Cats to the Tennessee 22-yard line. The late Claude Sullivan calls UK's next play.

SULLIVAN CALL: "Don Netoskie flanks right...Hardy calls his play...now they give him yardage...he rolls out, he's gonna throw...he stays right...he looks for his man...he's got one wide open on the left side of the field...it's Schnellenberger...he catches it and he's over for a touchdown...Howie Schnellenberger, how about that!"

LEDFORD: That touchdown tied the score 13-all. Delmar Hughes came on to kick the crucial extra point. Billy Mitchell was to hold. Again, Sullivan calls the action.

SULLIVAN CALL: "Here's the snap...the placement is down...Hughes kicks...it's good!"

LEDFORD: The 10,000 Kentucky fans who had made the trip to Knoxville were in a frenzy. Their beloved Cats had finally beaten the Vols in Neyland Stadium. What those fans didn't know was that the Cats had won it on a broken play. Schellenberger described the play as he remembered it.

SCHNELLENBERGER: "Bob made his fake to Bob Dougherty over tackle and then rolled out slightly to his right looking for Bradley Mills or Dick Maloney or somebody over there on the right side, strong side. Tennessee had defensed it well and had covered it. I blocked my man — I don't remember who he was — I blocked him as long as I could. I fell down in the mud and I don't know if he fell and got up and started chasing the play, but I didn't chase the play, I just kind of got up and saw that the halfback on my side had revolved over to the other side out of instinct, I guess. I didn't run a long way, I just backed away from where everybody was. It took a long time. Bob looked and looked and looked downfield for Mills and Maloney and those guys. Finally, he looked back across the field and threw the ball."

LEDFORD: The ball sailed wobbly across the rain-soaked field until it nestled safely into Howard's hands. Then it became a foot race to the goal line, a race Schnellenberger would win to give the Cats the victory.

ROCKIN' THE REBELS

(The University of Kentucky football Wildcats have scored many big wins down through the years, but few were bigger or more glorious than the one that took place Sept. 26, 1964. On that sunny afternoon in Jackson, Miss., Charlie Bradshaw's Wildcats bumped off the top-ranked Ole Miss Rebels, 27-21.)

LEDFORD: In 1964, Kentucky opened the football season with a disappointing 13-6 win over a mediocre Detroit team. The next week found the Wildcats in Jackson, Miss., to take on the Ole Miss Rebels. Ole Miss had won two-straight Southeastern Conference championships, and was, at the time, ranked No. 1 in the nation. Rick Kestner was an end on that Kentucky team and had perhaps his greatest game, hauling in three touchdown passes. According to Rick, the Cats came out with fire in their eyes that afternoon, only to shoot themselves in the foot during the early going. Rick remembers one peculiar play.

KESTNER: "The play was really supposed to be a running play to Rodger Bird, but Rodger had nowhere to go and had to circle back around. He was going to the right and he circled back around to the left. He spotted Tom Becherer open about 20 yards downfield and threw the ball to Tom Becherer. There wasn't anybody close to him except Tony Manzonelli, our left offensive tackle."

LEDFORD: The touchdown was called back...ineligible receiver downfield. Still, Kentucky drove all the way to the Ole Miss 16. That's when the Cats shot themselves in the foot once again. Quarterback Rick Norton put the ball in the air, only to have it picked off.

KESTNER: "Jimmy Heidle intercepted the pass and ran it

back 90 yards for a touchdown. That put us behind 7-0."

LEDFORD: Norton atoned for his miscue by scoring on a keeper to tie the score at 7-7. The Cats were off to the races after that. Bird, a halfback, improvised again later in the game, hitting Kestner for a touchdown pass. This time there were no ineligible receivers downfield. The Cats eventually upped their lead over the heavily favored Rebels to 27-21, but Ole Miss had the ball and was moving. The Cats needed a big play defensively if they were to hang on for the upset win. And that's exactly what they got, thanks to Jim Foley and Talbott Todd.

KESTNER: "Jim Foley hit Mike Dennis. Mike went one way and the ball went straight up in the air. Talbott Todd recovered the fumble in the air. Talbott was tackled, and I remember as the clock ticked down we just couldn't believe we'd beaten the No. 1 team in the nation."

LEDFORD: It was a great Wildcat victory. While the players were in wild celebration, the dressing room door opened and legendary Ole Miss coach Johnny Vaught walked in. He asked to speak to the UK team. Kestner remembers Vaught's words.

KESTNER: "Coach Vaught said, 'I've been around football all of my life. I'm 60-some-odd-years old and that is the greatest exhibition of football between two teams that I've ever seen. You all are the more courageous team and wanted it more than we did. It is the greatest victory I've ever seen by anybody.' "

LEDFORD: It was a day for celebrating, yet the biggest celebration was to come later when the Cats landed back in Lexington.

KESTNER: "They couldn't even taxi the airplane to the terminal. There was something like 20,000 people at Bluegrass Field. They were parking all the way into Keeneland's parking lot, they were all over the runway and it was absolute bedlam at Bluegrass Field. It was the most fantastic thing I've ever seen in my life. I've never seen anything like it since."

LEDFORD: Rick Kestner went on to have many magnificent moments as a football player, but it was that long ago day in Jackson that will always burn the brightest in his memory.

The victorious Wildcats, 27-21 upset winners over No. 1 Ole Miss, returned to a jam-packed throng at Bluegrass Airport.

HECK OF A DAY

(Kentucky's last victory over Tennessee on the football field occurred on Nov. 24, 1984 in Knoxville. Bill Ransdell, a sophomore quarterback for the Cats at the time, played a huge role in helping UK spoil the party for the Tennessee faithful.)

LEDFORD: More than 94,000 fans were on hand to watch that 1984 war between the two ancient rivals. It was the largest crowd to ever watch the Cats and Vols in action. Kentucky entered the game with a 7-3 record. Tennessee was 6-2-1. Quarterback Bill Ransdell remembers the importance of that game.

RANSDELL: "Definitely, there were bowl aspirations, but nobody had really given us a good look. If I had to guess, I'd say the coaches knew before the game that if we win, we go, and that if Tennessee wins, they go, which is what happened. We didn't know it, but they supposedly had all their stuff set up at the Tennessee place because they thought they were going to win."

LEDFORD: The talented Vols were led by a great quarterback named Tony Robinson. Robinson was a multi-dimensional player who could hurt opponents in a variety of ways. Ransdell says the key to a Kentucky victory was containing the flashy Robinson.

RANSDELL: "The big thing we wanted to do was to keep Tony in the pocket, make him throw the ball. That put a lot of pressure on our defensive secondary, but we had to contain him as best we could. I mean, when you've got a player of his caliber, with that kind of speed and quickness, it's hard to do that."

LEDFORD: But the Cats did just that, and with Kentucky up 14-12 midway through the fourth quarter, UK lineman Jerry Reese broke through to sack Robinson. Here's how I called that big play by Reese.

LEDFORD CALL: "Back to throw is Robinson...Robinson scrambling off, running hard to his left...now he's being chased...he's hit and he fumbles it...it went out of bounds before Kentucky could get it...all the way back on the 35 as Jerry Reese went in and popped him."

LEDFORD: The sack forced the Vols into a third down and 16 situation. Once again, Reese forced Robinson into an intentional grounding call. The Vols had to punt. It gave the Cats the ball back with time to increase their two-point lead and a chance to milk the clock. Ransdell faced a tough third-and-eight from the Tennessee 45-yard line. With just under four minutes left, Ransdell stepped under center.

LEDFORD CALL: "Tennessee's coming with the blitz...Ransdell's rolling right, rolling, throwing...great catch by Joker Phillips down on the 35...that'll be a first down."

LEDFORD: After that, kicker Joey Worley added a 33-yard field goal to put Kentucky up 17-12. Robinson led his team back down the field in the closing minutes, but a final desperation pass fell incomplete in the end zone as time expired. Neyland Stadium was silent, except for the screams of joy coming from the Kentucky fans who had just witnessed one of the biggest Wildcat wins in history...a win that clinched the Cats a berth in the Hall of Fame Bowl.

RANSDELL: "It was a heck of a day. God Almighty it was. It made the drive back easy too."

BOWL WIN

(Kentucky's last bowl victory on the gridiron took place in 1984 in Birmingham, Ala. It was the Cats' second-straight trip to the Hall of Fame Bowl, but unlike the year before, the Cats came out on top in a thrilling 20-19 victory over Wisconsin. Former quarterback Bill Ransdell played a key role in that Wildcat victory.)

LEDFORD: Sophomore quarterback Bill Ransdell led the Wildcats to an 8-3 regular season record in the fall of '84. The last game, a 17-12 victory over Tennessee, earned Kentucky a repeat bid to the Hall of Fame Bowl in Birmingham to face Big Ten power Wisconsin. Ransdell remembers the night.

RANSDELL: "It was a beautiful night. I can remember the fireworks going off and us running out, our sidelines, our fans going crazy. Wisconsin had some big boys, I remember that. They had some huge guys."

LEDFORD: Those huge guys had one number in mind... No. 9, the jersey of Ransdell. They came at him with their ears pinned back. At the half, the Cats found themselves in the hole 16-7. Late in the third quarter, the Badgers led 19-10, but Kentucky had the ball on Wisconsin's 27-yard-line. The Cats needed a quick strike to get back into the game. Here's how I called what turned out to be a crucial play.

LEDFORD CALL: "Adams and Logan in the backfield...Phillips coming in motion to this side, the right side...Ransdell back to throw, oh and there is a pass to Logan...Logan gets a block, turns it upfield and he's at the 20, he's at the 10, he's at the five... knocked out of bounds...nope, touchdown!"

RANSDELL: "That was a huge play. They had been coming and coming and coming and it made them back off. They had to sit back and look and make sure we weren't going to do something like that again. It let them know we were there for real and we weren't gonna give up and pack our bags."

LEDFORD: And the Cats didn't quit. With 8:55 left in the game, Kentucky called on freshman kicker Joey Worley to attempt a school-record 52-yard field goal that would put the Cats on top.

Bill Ransdell's 27-yard touchdown strike to Mark Logan spearheaded UK's 20-19 come-from-behind 1984 Hall of Fame Bowl win.

LEDFORD CALL: "All right, let's see if they go through with it...Jones down on one knee, there's the snap, they're going to try it, and it is long enough...it is, I believe, yes, I think he got it...good!"

LEDFORD: Everyone held their breath as Worley's kick headed toward the uprights. Everyone, that is, except Bill Ransdell. He wasn't worried at all.

RANSDELL: "The reason I never looked at it is because, to me, Joey did such a hell of a job kicking the ball that I never thought about it. Once we got it there and we set it — and they decided to kick —I went back and got oxygen. I said this is no problem, it's through. I don't even remember. I can remember we were sitting up there and watching it, but it wasn't like I was going to come on really bad, because I had as much confidence in him as I've ever had in anything. I mean, he just knocked it through."

LEDFORD: Wisconsin had one last shot. With two minutes left, the Badgers had marched to the Kentucky eight-yard line. Time for a field goal try. It should have been a chip shot, and if successful, it would seal Kentucky's fate.

LEDFORD CALL: "It's just a 26-yarder...no, it's a fake...and here's Wisconsin scrambling around, still running, being chased in the backfield, and the holder throws it for the end zone...intercepted by the Wildcats in the end zone...I think that was a dumb play by Wisconsin."

LEDFORD: Actually, it was a bobbled snap and a nervous holder that led to the botched play. But for Kentucky, it was the end of perhaps the greatest comeback in UK history on the gridiron. Kentucky 20, Wisconsin 19.

GEORGE THE FIRST

(Former UK Wildcat George Blanda played in the National Football League from 1949 until 1975. During that span, he became the all-time leading scorer in the NFL.)

LEDFORD: George Blanda played at Kentucky from 1945 until 1948. He was the quarterback, punter, and place-kicker for the Big Blue. As a Wildcat, he was in on several firsts. He played on Paul "Bear" Bryant's first UK team. He played in Kentucky's first bowl game. And he was the career leader in punting average at Kentucky until 1984 when Paul Calhoun topped him. Blanda achieved greatness on the gridiron, and he traces that success back to his beginnings.

BLANDA: "Starting back growing up in Pennsylvania, all my brothers and my family and the little town I grew up in, you were almost expected to play football back then. After I got out of high school, certainly my biggest factor, probably why I was successful, was my association with Coach Bryant here at the University of Kentucky."

LEDFORD: Bear Bryant had been a head coach for only one year prior to taking the top post at Kentucky. Using his success at UK as a stepping stone, he went on to become one of the great football coaches of all-time. Blanda tells us what the early years with the Bear were like.

BLANDA: "He was very tough and difficult. It was right after World War II, I was an 18-year-old sophomore and we had all these returning servicemen 21-, 22-, 23-, 24-years of age. And the restrictions weren't as restrictive on the program as they are today. The NCAA didn't monitor it as closely as they probably should have and could have. We practiced football, you know, eternally. It seemed like it was a year-round job. He tried to run a lot of us off because really there was an overabundance of football players. But the players that survived were the best players."

LEDFORD: A new bowl game was created in 1947 and Kentucky received its first bowl invitation...to the Great Lakes Bowl in Cleveland, Ohio. To Blanda, that remains a cherished memory.

BLANDA: "It was a great experience even though back in those days there were only five bowl games. There was the Orange, Sugar, Cotton, the Rose Bowl and one other bowl. That was it. This was the start of the first new bowl games. In fact, the Gator Bowl was just starting that year. We chose to go to the Great Lakes Bowl because it didn't interfere with Christmas-time. To win that first bowl game for Coach Bryant was a great thrill. It got us started in the program, and the University on a winning track."

LEDFORD: Blanda scored six points in the Great Lakes Bowl to help Kentucky defeat Villanova, 24-14, and finish the 1947 season with a 9-3 record. His six points came on a field goal and three extra points. Who knew back in 1947 that Blanda's ability to kick the pigskin would keep him active for the next 26 years?

THE SWEET KENTUCKY BABE

(Vito "Babe" Parilli was voted the second greatest quarterback during the first 50 years of college football. He remains, to this day, the greatest quarterback in UK football history.)

LEDFORD: Babe Parilli first came to Lexington on a train from his hometown of Rochester, Pa., in 1946. He played for the Wildcats from 1949 until 1951, and in each of those three seasons, he led the Southeastern Conference in passing. In his final two seasons, the Babe earned All-American honors. He completed 56 percent of his passes during his career, while throwing for 50 touchdowns, which is still tops on UK's list. Despite those sterling accomplishments, Parilli wasn't recruited as a quarterback. He came to UK as a fullback, but his transition to quarterback came easily.

PARILLI: "Well, I threw the ball a lot, having been a passer in the single wing. Plus, I was very fortunate to have a guy like Ermal Allen here at the time. He was the quarterback coach and he taught me just about everything I know."

LEDFORD: After Parilli's glorious UK career, he played from 1952 until 1969 with five teams in the National Football League. And how would the Babe compare himself with the quarterbacks of today?

PARILLI: "I guess I might be a little undersized, but as far as throwing the ball, I don't think there's much difference. I think I had the foot quickness you need today. I know the pass rushes are pretty fierce today, but I think I could hold up to that. I would just say maybe a little undersized."

LEDFORD: Parilli played under one of the greatest football coaches of all time at Kentucky...Paul "Bear" Bryant. The

Babe says Bryant was a winner because of his unique style of coaching.

PARILLI: "I think there are different kinds of coaches and Coach Bryant had his way of coaching. I think he and (Vince) Lombardi were a lot alike. They both coached through fear. I think they got results that way. There is no patented way of coaching, but they were successful that way. I think he got the most out of his players by being that type of coach."

LEDFORD: Babe Parilli continues his football career as head coach of the Denver Dynamite in the Arena Football League. These days, he is teaching his great passing skills to his own quarterbacks. Although he played for two of the game's greatest coaches, Parilli says he seldom uses their style.

PARILLI: "I do to an extent, but I try to coach my way. I think you have to be your own person. You can't copy somebody, because the players can see through that."

LEDFORD: Even though Parilli seldom returns to the Bluegrass, he will always be the measuring stick for UK quarterbacks. Luckily for Wildcat fans, his 1946 boxcar ride to Lexington turned out to be a one-way trip. The Sweet Kentucky Babe...still UK's greatest.

CHALLENGING THE BEAR

(The pinnacle of UK football came in 1951 when the Wildcats stunned unbeaten and top-ranked Oklahoma in the Sugar Bowl. Bob Gain, a senior that season, was a key figure in that game.)

LEDFORD: Bob Gain was a two-time All-America selection in 1949 and 1950. After his senior year in 1950, he was awarded the prestigious Outland Trophy for his outstanding interior lineman play. During his days at UK, Gain had many great moments, but when you ask the Weirton, W.Va., native to name his most memorable moment, he says it's no contest.

GAIN: "Winning the Sugar Bowl and making restitution for the defeat we had that 1950 season down in Knoxville."

LEDFORD: The 1950 Wildcats were one of the greatest UK teams ever assembled. Kentucky was 10-0 with one game left to play in its regular season...a game against arch-rival Tennessee in Knoxville. The Volunteers' deadly spell over Kentucky continued that November day as Tennessee recorded a 7-0 shutout. The Wildcats were still Southeastern Conference Champions, but a cloud was cast over Kentucky's locker room that afternoon.

GAIN: "Bear Bryant wanted to go back to the Orange Bowl, but the seniors did not want to go back to the Orange Bowl. The only way we felt we could make restitution for our loss that particular day against Tennessee was to come back and play the best in the country, which was Oklahoma."

LEDFORD: Coach Bryant had wanted to go back to the Orange Bowl because the previous season, the Wildcats had lost there to Santa Clara 21-13. Plus, the game in Miami had a larger monetary value to Kentucky than any other bowl at that time. Yet the 27 seniors stood firm against the Bear and said no.

GAIN: "So he went out there and he said, 'I don't know if I can get Oklahoma and if I can get the Sugar Bowl.' And I said, 'Well, the season's over.' So he came back a little later and told us that he got us Oklahoma in the Sugar Bowl."

LEDFORD: As they were throughout the 1980s, the 1950 Oklahoma Sooners were feared on the gridiron. The Cats wanted to mend their disappointing loss to Tennessee with a victory over the nation's best. According to Gain, the Bear was more than a little worried. And the UK players? Gain says they were pumped.

GAIN: "Losing to Tennessee that day probably gave us the motivation to play well over our heads, to give that 110 percent."

LEDFORD: After it was over, the headlines read "Kentucky 13, Oklahoma 7." The players had achieved just what they wanted — restitution for the loss to Tennessee by defeating the nation's top team. As usual, Bob Gain played both sides of the line of scrimmage. He also connected on one of two point-after attempts. The Cats have never had another season like the one they had in 1950. Perhaps that's because they haven't had many players like Bob Gain.

THE GREAT LOU

(Some say he was the greatest football player to ever wear the blue and white of Kentucky, and that no Wildcat before or since could single-handedly dominate a game like he could. His name...Lou Michaels.)

LEDFORD: Lou Michaels was a two-time All-America selection who hailed from Swoyerville, Pa. He was a fierce and determined athlete who hated to lose. Lou Michaels played tackle at Kentucky. He also served as punter and place-kicker. Actually, he played just about anywhere he wanted. Tennessee coach Johnny Majors once said that Lou Michaels was the toughest player he ever saw. To Lou, it's all in how you approach the game.

MICHAELS: "I didn't like the word lose...it disgusts me to the bitter end. Anytime I compete, and I'm still playing softball at the age of 55, I don't like the idea of losing. Along with this comes the desire — the bitter desire — to win."

LEDFORD: Michaels played at Kentucky under Blanton Collier from 1955 through 1957. His performances led him to win numerous awards throughout the South, including the *Nashville Banner's* Outstanding Player of the Year Award his senior year. Yet, despite the success that came his way, things weren't always easy for Michaels while he was growing up.

MICHAELS: "I was just a pure, lucky individual who came from a home that had little. You know, we had seven boys and one girl. We struggled very often...didn't have too much to eat, so when I got this opportunity to get a free scholarship and get to school, hey, I loved it here."

LEDFORD: In 1957, Kentucky was playing the top-ranked

Auburn Tigers in Auburn. With the game still scoreless, Michaels committed a personal foul. He was called for, of all things, tackling too hard. Here's how he explains it.

MICHAELS: "Tony Lorino, I spun out of a double-team on the left side and I chased him and he cut back and I ran completely over him. He fumbled the ball, we recovered it, the fans booed and the officials threw a flag and said that's illegal. Don't know what it was, but they gave him the football back and penalized us 15 yards."

LEDFORD: The Cats ended up losing the game 6-0 to the eventual conference champions. But it was that type of motivation and intensity that made Michaels hated by opposing coaches, players and officials. He firmly believes the athletes of today are lacking that kind of intense desire to win.

MICHAELS: "Attitudes are getting poorer and poorer. I see my kids, the younger generation, they take a loss like it's nothing. But you've got to remember, you've got to sit down and look back, look at your life and say maybe if I won this or I won that or I did this or I did that it might have been better. That's why I'm saying you've got to instill the desire to win, and if you can put this in a football player, I guarantee you, you will be the best."

LEDFORD: The desire to win was evident from the way Lou Michaels played the game. He was as tough as they come. For Kentucky, he was the best.

BIG SAM

(Henderson native Sam Ball was an All-American offensive lineman for the Wildcats and a Super Bowl winner with the Baltimore Colts. Big Sam, who joined the UK broadcast crew this season, was also Bill Curry's teammate on the Colts.)

LEDFORD: Sam Ball says he came to UK because the guys at Bobby Ward's gas station in Henderson told him it was the only place to go. When Sam arrived at UK, he found himself surrounded by a ton of football talent. Yet, despite a roster that included the likes of Rodger Bird, Rick Norton, Rick Kestner, Bob Windsor and Larry Seiple, the Cats achieved only so-so success. Ball says there's a reason why.

BALL: "We had three All-Americans and four first-round draft choices all on the offensive unit. I don't know if that's ever happened before, if that has happened at UK or anywhere else since then, but that's a colossal amount of talent on one unit on a college football team. We were loaded on offense and pretty mediocre on defense. I tell people probably the reason that we couldn't have been better is because (Coach Charlie) Bradshaw ran off some phenomenal talent, guys like Maurice Mooreman, Dale Lindsey. Because of that, our numbers were down."

LEDFORD: Sam earned consensus All-America honors as a tackle in 1965. He then went on to spend the next five years with the Colts. Along the way, he played in two Super Bowls, including the 1971 game in which the Colts beat Dallas 16-13 for the title. Sam says playing in the Super Bowl is an awesome experience.

BALL: "When you play in the Super Bowl, the night before, the night you lay your head down to go to bed and the next day when you get up and you're playing for the world championship, that's when it really, really dawns on you."

LEDFORD: Probably no person in Kentucky knows Bill Curry better than Sam Ball. The two were teammates on the Colts for four years. In fact, Ball says, they were more than just teammates.

BALL: "Not only were we teammates, we were on the same line of scrimmage. I tell people when the Fearsome Foursome came to town, there were five guys charged with stopping that business. And the same when the Purple People Eaters came to town, or the Doomsday Defense of the Dallas Cowboys. Not only did I play with Bill Curry, but on the same line of scrimmage. I've got a great admiration and love for Bill Curry. He's my friend, he's my brother."

LEDFORD: And how does Ball think his ex-teammate will do as UK's head man?

BALL: "He'll do great. He's a super coach, and if people will just be patient with him a little bit until he gets all his systems in place and goes out and recruits and finds the players he needs to win with, Bill Curry will make a major, major mark at UK football."

LEDFORD: This football season is a special one for Sam Ball...his son, Shane, is a redshirt freshman linebacker for the Wildcats.

BALL: "My son playing for Kentucky is just unbelievable, and having him play for Bill Curry at Kentucky is just like super icing on the cake. I love it."

LEDFORD: Sam Ball still lives in Henderson, where he's a successful businessman. In recent years, he's also become highly sought after as a motivational speaker. But it was down in the trenches, keeping opponents away from Rick Norton and Johnny Unitas, that Sam Ball carved out his legacy.

Sam Ball, a former All-American tackle at Kentucky, is now a successful businessman, a popular motivational speaker and color analyst for the UK Football Television Network.

SIMPLY THE BEST

(Sonny Collins is still regarded by many as the greatest running back in University of Kentucky history. He owns numerous records, and he set those standards by combining power, speed and acceleration.)

LEDFORD: Sonny Collins came to the University of Kentucky after a brilliant career at Madisonville High School. When he left UK four years later, he was the all-time leader in rushing and in all-purpose yards. Those records still stand today, but Collins doesn't think they'll last much longer.

COLLINS: "I'm really surprised that there are a few records of mine that are still standing. But I also feel that with Bill Curry here, knowing Coach Curry and his scenario, that he will have some great running backs coming to Kentucky. It's going to be exciting around here for all of us. And, of course, those running backs he'll recruit will be able to start breaking these kind of records that were set 15 years ago."

LEDFORD: Six of UK's 13 best rushing performances were turned in by Sonny Collins. His best effort came in 1973 when he rushed for 229 yards against Mississippi State. Collins says that performance resulted from going against standard operating procedure.

COLLINS: "We ran the veer, which meant we were pretty good off-tackle and running the sweeps. Of course, our opponents would always adjust to our offense. Usually, they shifted just the opposite way that I lined up. In other words, if I was behind the offensive tackle, the left opposite tackle, normally we would sweep to the right. They would shift the defense completely to the strong side of our offense. I can recall that Coach (Fran) Curci said there's only one man on the left side that Sonny's lined up against and we've got a guard and tackle. The one man they had was the defensive end."

LEDFORD: As a running back, Collins had it all...the speed to outrun a defensive back and the power to run over a linebacker. Surprisingly, Collins says athletic ability wasn't his greatest asset as a football player.

COLLINS: "Love of the game, enjoying what I was doing and, of course, when I signed here with the University of Kentucky it was what I had always dreamed of. And when I came here, I believed not only in the program here but also what I wanted to do."

LEDFORD: Collins has been familiar with the UK football program for a long time. He understands the frustration of those fans who want to see the football Cats do well. And he thinks the program is about to take that step forward.

COLLINS: "I think they've taken that step. Of course, Coach (Jerry) Claiborne had done a tremendous job, there's no question about that, but I think they turned up the notch about 20-fold when they signed Coach Curry to this program."

LEDFORD: Bill Curry is the right man to take UK football to a higher level, and if he can bring in a few running backs like Sonny Collins, he'll get the Cats there in a hurry.

A LINEBACKER'S WORST NIGHTMARE

(Joe Federspiel had a distinguished career as a football player. He was a standout linebacker at UK and later in the NFL. Federspiel is currently an SEC official.)

LEDFORD: When you start talking about great linebackers at the University of Kentucky, the name Joe Federspiel has to be near the top. A two-time All-SEC performer, Joe was one of the toughest defenders to ever wear the blue and white. But his tough brand of defense didn't stop after he graduated from UK. Joe went on to spend the next 10 years in the NFL. As a pro, he faced all the great running backs. That brings up the question...what's a linebacker's worst nightmare?

FEDERSPIEL: "The situation a pro linebacker, or especially a middle linebacker, really dreads is being one-on-one with a big fullback or a halfback in the open field. Normally, middle linebackers are not your most agile players on defense, but they are your big hitters. When you get isolated one-on-one with a very quick, speedy back, or a big back, then all of a sudden you know you've got to make the tackle. You've got to bring him down in the open field and you really don't have that support you have when you're in the middle. So that would be my worst nightmare."

LEDFORD: As a middle linebacker, Joe usually faced head-on with the opposing center. Federspiel remembers playing against one center in particular...UK coach Bill Curry.

FEDERSPIEL: "Bill and I tangled a couple of times before he actually retired, I think, back in 1974. I remember Bill when he was an offensive center for the Houston Oilers. It was sort of the twilight of his career, but he was still a very vigorous football player. I remember him in particular because I got a couple of good shots on him. I still tease him about the time that I got him real good, and about two plays later, he got me real good. I still complain about that knot he left on my shin with that leg whip he put on me one year."

LEDFORD: Joe's appreciation of Bill Curry's toughness isn't limited to what happened during those NFL days...it has carried over to the job Curry is doing as UK's coach. Joe predicts good things ahead for the UK program.

FEDERSPIEL: "I think Bill Curry has brought a lot of enthusiasm to the program. Anytime you have a change and you've got a coach like Coach Curry and his staff, it generates excitement. I think that Coach Curry's work ethic, and the way he applies his teaching to the players, I think it's going to make these players play a little bit better than they really are. With the schedule they have this year, they could have a real big year."

LEDFORD: Joe Federspiel didn't forget his alma mater when he finished his playing days. He's still an active supporter of the University of Kentucky. He has also remained active in the sport he loves so much.

FEDERSPIEL: "Right now, I'm selling insurance here in the Lexington-Fayette County area. During the football season, I officiate SEC games. So, yes, I'm still very much involved in football, following the Wildcats and officiating on Saturday afternoons."

LEDFORD: Joe Federspiel is precisely the kind of individual any university is proud to claim. He was an asset to UK when he played, and he still is today.

TWO-WAY STANDOUT

(Former UK coach Jerry Claiborne preached endlessly on how important the kicking game was to winning. It was never more important than against Mississippi State in 1984 when Paul Calhoun's strong right leg led the Cats to victory.)

LEDFORD: When Paul Calhoun graduated from UK in 1984, he left behind many punting records. The most outstanding was a 42.5 yards per punt career average. Paul turned in a host of splendid performances, but none was more splendid than the one that came against Mississippi State on Oct. 13, 1984. His kicking led directly to that Wildcat victory. Here's how I called a booming first-half punt by Calhoun that was a tip-off to what lay ahead.

LEDFORD CALL: "Here's the kick, and it is a beauty...it's a long spinner...backing up is Lundy...he takes it on the five...he goes back out to the 10 and gets a block...he's still on his feet...he shakes the tackler, gets to the 25 and there he is brought down by Tony Mayes."

LEDFORD: Calhoun's punt covered 62 yards, his longest of the day. Overall, Calhoun had eight punts for a 50-yard average. However, the biggest play he made all day was a punt he didn't kick. It was a fake punt, similar to the one he had scored on earlier in the year against Indiana. This time, the Cats weren't afraid. They were down 13-10 with less than 10 minutes to go and they were looking for something to happen. Here's how I called Calhoun's heroic play.

LEDFORD CALL: "There's no rush at all...Calhoun's gonna run it...he's down to the 30...he gets to the 35, heads off to the right, shakes a tackle at the 40...he's still on his feet...he's all the way out to midfield...that might be the break the Cats need...Paul Calhoun looked, saw no rush coming, and he runs Kentucky out into this game."

LEDFORD: Calhoun was astonished that Mississippi State would retreat so easily. When they did, Coach Claiborne said all he wanted to do was yell, "Run!, Run!" But he didn't have to. Calhoun was already on his horse.

CALHOUN: "Mississippi State did the same thing as Indiana. I looked up and checked where the rush was coming from and I saw that every one of them was gone. There wasn't a single man left there, so I ended up taking off, running again, doing the same thing, taking the hops and skips, waiting for somebody to come."

LEDFORD: His sprint from his own 26 to midfield wasn't planned. It wasn't planned the first time he tried it against Indiana either. But the big play came as a surprise to the senior.

CALHOUN: "Indiana didn't do it (rush) and it surprised me that nobody would check to make sure the punter punted that ball. Once it happened before, you would assume that most teams would be aware of it, so that's what really caught me by surprise, that I thought surely they would be checking."

LEDFORD: Spurred by Paul's effort, quarterback Bill Ransdell then led the Cats to the winning touchdown. It was Paul's superior punting job, combined with his solid defensive contributions at safety, that led Kentucky to a 5-0 record...its best start since 1950.

CALHOUN: "Most games I'd either play good at defensive back and have an OK day punting, or I'd have a great day punting and play so-so at defensive back. That was one game I was able to put both together."

LEDFORD: He kept them both together, ending his career as the leading punter in UK modern-day history. He also ended the 1984 campaign with seven interceptions — second only to Claiborne's nine interceptions for a season in 1949. Paul Calhoun...one of the most versatile players ever at UK.

One of the most versatile players in UK gridiron history, Paul Calhoun earned All-SEC honors as a punter and defensive back during the 1984 campaign.

CURRY'S MAGIC TOUCH

(Kentucky has long been noted for its fast horses...those beautiful thoroughbreds that run for the roses each May. UK football coach Bill Curry and his staff want the fans to think of speed in a different context...Kentucky football. If his first two recruiting classes are any indication, then he's well on his way to making that happen.)

LEDFORD: The national signing period for college football has just concluded, and on paper at least, it looks as though UK Coach Bill Curry has brought in a wealth of talent. To him, this successful harvest was expected. To UK fans, it was a total surprise. The height, weight and speed these future Wildcats possess is just what the doctor ordered. It's a group that appears to have the potential to someday rank among the top recruiting classes to arrive in Lexington. UK has always had difficulty recruiting the true blue-chip players. Why, then, did this talented group choose the Big Blue? Bill Curry thinks he has the answer.

CURRY: "I think the family atmosphere here made it final for an awful lot of them. I think if you had to pick one characteristic other than the obvious, that we have a great University here, it would be the family atmosphere we provide. I would hope that's the reason that all of them came. But when it gets down to those things that are gut-level feelings, you go around and you visit the different schools, trying to figure out where am I going to feel good about myself, I believe what they felt here is so authentic."

LEDFORD: Curry's long recruiting arm could be seen in virtually every part of the country, but it was especially visible in the Southeast. It was there that he tapped the talent well at many of the real high school powerhouses. Leon Smith from

Louisville Trinity, Stephen Langenkamp from Cincinnati Moeller and James Tucker from Arlington Lamar High in Texas are just a few of the recruits who come from big-time prep programs. Curry says shopping these high schools will help his program in the future.

CURRY: "When these guys go back home, the coaches pull them aside and say, 'All right, do they really tutor you the way they said? Are they really giving you a chance? What's your schedule like? How are you treated? Are you treated with dignity? Is that family thing that you thought you felt, is that real?' And those coaches get a feel for the program. If they get a good feeling, then the next player they have, if you want to recruit him, the coach is not going to send him to you, but he will help you to get visits and that sort of thing. Then you have to do your own recruiting."

LEDFORD: That's not the only benefit from recruiting the top prep programs. There's another benefit of equal importance...a winning attitude. Take Leon Smith from Louisville Trinity. He never lost a game at the varsity level.

CURRY: "Those programs traditionally turn out great players, but they also turn out players who know how to win. If you have a vast majority of your players who are accustomed to winning, guys like Leon Smith — has he ever played a losing game? — those guys understand what it takes to win, so they come in, they're ready to get to work toward winning. You don't have to teach them how to win. You just teach them how to catch the ball or how to work their class schedule or whatever. That's why it's crucial that we focus on those programs."

LEDFORD: How good was UK's recruiting year? Curry says he'll let us know the answer to that in three years. He says that's how long it takes before you can really evaluate any recruiting class. However, those experts who closely monitor the recruiting scene rate this UK class as one of the best nationally, especially since Curry signed Damon Hood. According to them, Curry and his staff struck gold.

Kentucky football coach Bill Curry hopes his first two Wildcat recruiting classes are an indication of good things to come for UK gridiron fortunes.

BIG RED

(No horse in recent years captured the public's affection like Secretariat. From the day he won the Kentucky Derby until his death, Secretariat was the fans' favorite.)

LEDFORD: They called him "Big Red of Meadow Stable" and he was one of the greatest race horses of all-time. Also, one of the most popular. The great Secretariat. Secretariat had been "Horse of the Year" as a two-year-old, the first juvenile so acclaimed. In 1973, Seth Hancock of Claiborne Farm syndicated Secretariat for a then-record $6 million plus. Despite the big bucks, Secretariat came to the Kentucky Derby fresh from a less-than-impressive third-place finish in the Wood Memorial. That would, however, turn out to be Secretariat's last poor race. The colt they called the "Big Train" was to run a big, big Derby. Here's how I called it down the stretch.

LEDFORD CALL: "All right, here it is...Sham on the inside...Secretariat on the outside...and it's Angle Light in third...it's Sham on the inside...Secretariat on the outside...Angle Light trying to hold third...Secretariat has the lead...he's got less than 150 yards to come...and Secretariat is on top and he's going to take it all!"

LEDFORD: He took it by two-and-a-half lengths, running the fastest Derby to this day — one-minute-59-and-two-fifth seconds. The flashy chestnut went on to win the Preakness and the Belmont. John Sosby, manager of Claiborne Farm where Secretariat was to spend his career in stud, remembers being tremendously impressed by Big Red's blazing win in the Belmont.

SOSBY: "I'll never forget it. I've seen it two dozen times since then, and every time I see it, the goose bumps come up on my arm, because it's the greatest race I've ever seen."

LEDFORD: Here's celebrated racing announcer Chic Anderson's famous call of those final moments of the Belmont.

ANDERSON CALL: "Secretariat is widening it now...he is coming like a tremendous machine...Secretariat by 12...Secretariat by 14 lengths on the turn...Sham is dropping back...it looks like they'll catch him (Sham) today...My Gallant and Twice the Prince are both coming up to him now...but Secretariat is all alone...he's out there almost a 16th of a mile away from the rest of the horses."

LEDFORD: When Secretariat hit the finish line, he was an amazing 31 lengths ahead of his nearest competitor. It was a world-record victory, and it gave thoroughbred racing its first Triple Crown winner in a quarter of a century. After Secretariat retired and moved to Claiborne Farm, he was overshadowed by some of the great stallions at Claiborne. But nothing could diminish his appeal with the fans. Until the day he was put down, Secretariat remained the peoples' horse.

SOSBY: "Of the, say, 8,500 people that would tour at Claiborne every year, 90 to 95 percent of those people would want to see Secretariat. Of all the horses I've ever seen in my life, and I've seen thousands of them pass through Claiborne in one stage or another, he, Secretariat, is the prettiest horse I ever saw."

LEDFORD: In October 1989, the 1973 Triple Crown Winner, the great Secretariat was gone, and his untimely death triggered a hero's response from his legion of fans.

SOSBY: "The number of flowers, 106 different arrangements the next day or during that afternoon or the next morning when we were able to open the grave to the general public, and the news media was incredible. Again, 106 different arrangements of flowers, from one single rose to an elaborate spray."

LEDFORD: Secretariat was one of the true giants of the turf. Those thoroughbreds who have followed him, and those yet to come will always be measured against the legendary Big Red.

The Triple Crown winner in 1973, Secretariat will always be remembered for his remarkable, 31-length win at the Belmont Stakes.

THE SMALL GIANT

(Pat Day has become one of the top jockeys in thoroughbred racing. He's won three Eclipse Awards and four riding titles, while winning more than 5,000 races.)

LEDFORD: Pat Day was raised on a ranch in Colorado. He got his start around horses while participating in rodeos, but it didn't take long before his size had him primed to be a race rider. Now he's one of the top riders in the sport, so I asked him how much of a difference a rider makes in a race. Pat said the answer to that question can vary from race to race, and to prove his point, he turned to the victories jockey Jerry Bailey had in the Belmont and the Mother Goose Stakes earlier in 1991.

DAY: "I think he contributed greatly to the victory. Now, I'm not saying there weren't some other riders in the country who couldn't have got the job done, but on that afternoon, his contribution was great. By the same token, I don't know that he contributed all that much in his victory in the Jim Beam aboard Hansel. Hansel was so much the best that day, as in the Preakness, as in the Lexington, but his victory in the Belmont, I think Jerry certainly was a major factor."

LEDFORD: You often hear trainers talk about strategy during a race. Where to keep the horse early. When to make the move. All trainers and jockeys study their competition. It's essential that they know strengths and weaknesses before formulating a game plan. However, even the best of plans can change when the starting gate opens. Pat gives this example.

DAY: "You might go into a race figuring that there's two or three legitimate speed horses. Your horse might be a speed horse but you decide this particular day, between you and your trainer, that the other speeds should burn themselves out and you should lay third or fourth. Then when the gates open, you're on the lead and everybody else is laying back. What do you do? You understand what I'm saying? At that point in time, it's like the play has fallen apart, you're left holding the ball and you've got to run. It's like football. I think what separates the great running backs from the so-so running backs are those that have the ability, when the play falls apart, to ad-lib and get the job done."

LEDFORD: So the jockeys have to adapt. But is that what separates the great riders from the good riders?

DAY: "I think what separates the great riders from the good riders is that the great riders make fewer mistakes. First of all, you have be on the stock. You can't drive a Volkswagen in a Cadillac race and expect to win. However, there are times when Volkswagens win Cadillac races, you know? I mean, it's just a matter of racing luck. You know, the best horse doesn't always win. The great riders make fewer mistakes, in my opinion."

LEDFORD: Well, your opinion counts Pat Day. It counts because you are one of the great riders in the history of thoroughbred racing.

DERBY CONVERT

(Few people within the horse racing community need to be converted when it comes to the importance of the Kentucky Derby. Jack Price is one such man.)

LEDFORD: In 1961, an outrageous little man came to Churchill Downs insisting the Derby was just another horse race. Jack Price was the man, and as you might expect, his feelings about the Derby sent all Kentuckians' blood pressure up a few notches. Even after his horse, Carry Back, won the Run for the Roses, Price still insisted the Derby was just another horse race.

PRICE: "I deprecated the Derby. When I was here, they said they ought to take Jack Price and tar and feather him and run him out of Louisville."

LEDFORD: What infuriated Kentuckians even more was that Jack Price meant it. To him, it was just another horse race. On May 6, 1961, the favored Carry Back broke from post position 14 in the 15-horse field. Price instructed jockey Johnny Sellers to lay about 10 lengths off the lead, but going down the backstretch, Carry Back had fallen far behind. Sellers was to tell Jack after the race that he saw three horses up on the front end, but when he caught up to them, there were another three horses still ahead. Carry Back had an awful lot of ground to make up.

PRICE: "At the head of the stretch, he was nearly 15 lengths out of it. He really thrilled the crowd with his final run. He thrilled me too."

LEDFORD: Here's my call of Carry Back's thrilling stretch run.

LEDFORD CALL: "Grozier is out in front...Carry Back has moved into second...the others can't keep up...it's going to be an old grudge between these two...and Carry Back comes on...he's got him...and they're running head and head...and here comes Carry Back to pick off the win...wins it by three-parts of a length...Grozier second."

LEDFORD: Carry Back had his Kentucky Derby, yet Jack Price left Louisville still contending that the Derby was just another horse race. However, it didn't take long for that to change. Jim Bolus, who has written two books about the Derby and is a great friend to Price, explains.

BOLUS: "It took him a while, I think, to realize the impact of that race. Now he's become the Derby's greatest fan. I don't know of any other owner who has come back to the Derby every year since winning the Derby, yet Jack's done that. He's been very faithful to the Derby."

LEDFORD: Jack Price recalls his change of heart.

PRICE: "I never thought it would be the way it was. You know, we won a lot of races before the Derby and big races too. The pots were bigger than the Derby pot. But when you tell people that you won the richest race in the world, like the Garden State, they say, 'Well, gee, The Garden State, what's that?' When you tell them you trained and owned the winner of the Kentucky Derby, they, like, genuflect."

LEDFORD: Jack Price is truly a friend of the Kentucky Derby. In his 80s now, he still finds time to get back to Churchill Downs for that first Saturday in May. He visits with old acquaintances. And he visits another old friend. Carry Back is buried at Churchill Downs. And, no doubt, Jack Price reminisces about that great long ago day when Carry Back forever changed Jack's feelings about the Run for the Roses.

THE $10 HORSE

(Judy Hicks went to college with one thing in mind...to work with thoroughbred race horses. Her dream came true for just $10. That's right, 10 one dollar bills.)

LEDFORD: All it takes is one horse and some land to start a horse farm. Usually though, it takes more than just one horse to make it successful. But Judy Hicks proved to be the exception to the rule. How did she get started, you ask?

HICKS: "I came to Kentucky about 10 years ago, working as an intern up at Forest Retreat Farm. My goal was to learn everything there was to learn about horses. After doing a course at Texas A&M in horse production, instead of writing a thesis, I did this internship at Forest Retreat. Then I got right into a farm manager's job in Versailles. After that, I started my own feed business, a custom feed mixing for several of the local horse farms. Then I got my own farm and I started boarding horses."

LEDFORD: That's when Lady Luck made an appearance. One of the owners Judy was boarding for didn't pay his bills. That left Judy with two yearlings, but no way to collect on the outstanding debt. It was time for her to act.

HICKS: "I was allowed to hold a sale, and in Kentucky you have to advertise it like any other auction. I held the sale, but the only person who showed up was the sheriff. I had these $2,000 thoroughbred yearlings, so I asked the sheriff how much do I have to pay you so I own them. And he said, 'I don't know, something, $4, $5, $10,' so I looked in my pocket and I had $20, so I gave him $10 for the filly and $10 for the colt."

LEDFORD: The filly has turned out to be a gem although Judy first had trouble getting her registered with the Jockey Club. You see, the filly's mare had died before a blood typing was done, leaving the filly unregistered. So after much red tape — notarized statements and such — The Jockey Club passed the registration. The filly is Phoenix Sunshine, and now as a six-year-old, she's earned nearly $200,000 on the track. Recently, she ran in the Bewitch Stakes at Keeneland. Soon she'll be defending the Mint Julep Trophy she won last year at Churchill Downs. And before you know it, Judy will be breeding her to some of the top sires in racing.

HICKS: "I hope to breed her, probably next year. She will tell us when she's finished. It will probably be next year, and if she continues as she's going, I'll probably be able to breed her to anybody I want and have a July Keeneland yearling."

LEDFORD: All this for $10. Does Judy have any tips for would-be horse farmers on how to get started in the business?

HICKS: "I'd recommend people start going to these courthouse auctions because you never know what you might get."

LEDFORD: There aren't many Cinderella stories in the world of horse racing, but the story of Judy Hicks and her sawbuck filly certainly qualifies.

LUCKY JUNIOR

(Marvin Little Jr. grew up as a poor mountain boy in Paintsville, Ky. There's not much in his early biography to indicate future success in the thoroughbred industry, yet now, at age 53, he's bred a thoroughbred that fell just one race short of capturing the Triple Crown.)

LEDFORD: Marvin Little Jr., or just "Junior" to his friends, grew up without much in Paintsville. His early years weren't that different from other mountain kids. They didn't have much, but they endured.

LITTLE: "My daddy was blind and we lived off the land. We had a milk cow, we raised hogs, we raised a garden, my mother canned and there wasn't no such thing as welfare then. If she needed something like sugar, coffee, she got a couple a hens and took 'em to the poultry house in Paintsville and sold 'em for a few dollars to buy sugar, coffee, whatever. And I did go three years of high school."

LEDFORD: After those three years of high school, Little joined the Navy. Following his term in the service, he began working at Clovelly Farm in Bourbon County for $45 a week. It wasn't much pay, but it was a five-year period that got him started in the horse business.

LITTLE: "Lars LaCour, who really was the manager of Clovelly and still is, he taught me horses. And he had a whole building full of old horse and thoroughbred records, and I would take an armload of those home every night and read 'em from cover to cover. And everything I ever read about a horse went in there and stayed forever."

LEDFORD: He took what he learned with him to Newstead Farm in Virginia, where he served as farm manager. While he was there, he bought his first horse. It was an investment that almost put him back in the poor house.

LITTLE: "When I started to work at Clovelly, until 1980, which is 19 years, I saved a nickle and a dime at a time. My wife and I, we saved up $15,050. Then I went to Tumonium, Maryland. The first horse I ever owned, I bought Buenna Notte, the grand dam of Hansel, carrying Count on Bonnie for $15,000. A couple of weeks later we got the bill, which my wife immediately paid. She said to me, 'You son-of-a-gun, we've got five mouths to feed, we've got $50, and I can't even go to the grocery store.' "

LEDFORD: What may have been a questionable purchase at the time turned out to be one wise and lucky move. The mare produced just one foal, Count on Bonnie. After that, Marvin couldn't get her in foal again, so he gave her away. But he still had Count on Bonnie. Marvin bred her to Woodman, and that turned out to be the key to his success.

LITTLE: "The next spring, 1988, she had the most gorgeous foal I had ever seen. This was Hansel. I kept him until he was a yearling, then in September of his yearling year I sold him for $150,000. So I immediately got back all the money I'd tied up and used all those years, with a bunch left over."

LEDFORD: Marvin Little now has a full brother to Hansel that may end up being a Keeneland sales topper. That's not bad for a Paintsville boy named Junior.

HAPPY

(Former Kentucky Governor and Baseball Commissioner A.B. "Happy" Chandler passed away July 14 at the age of 92. He made his mark in many ways, but perhaps his greatest legacy was the role he played in integrating Major League Baseball by allowing Jackie Robinson to play for the Brooklyn Dodgers.)

LEDFORD: Happy Chandler is one of the most popular men this state has ever produced. After being elected to the senate, Happy left his office to take the job as Commissioner of Major League Baseball. It was during his tenure in that office that he made the decision that changed baseball forever. It was a decision that broke the color barrier and allowed blacks to play America's favorite pastime.

CHANDLER: "For 24 years, the record will show, of course, that my predecessor would not let the black man play. If you were black, you automatically were barred. They tried time after time and Judge Landis said to them, 'You're black, you can't play.' He wouldn't even let the white players barnstorm with the black fellas."

LEDFORD: In 1947, however, Brooklyn Dodgers' general manager Branch Rickey wanted to bring Jackie Robinson up to the big leagues. He needed a sympathetic ear, so he came to Versailles to meet with Happy.

CHANDLER: "In January of 1947, the owners, in a meeting over which I presided, voted 15-1 not to let Jackie Robinson play. Fifteen to one. As soon as that meeting was over, Branch Rickey, who had this boy signed to a Montreal contract, told me he was an outstanding player and that he wanted to bring him to Brooklyn. Rickey came down to my cabin, on the back side of my place in Versailles, and we talked for about an hour and a half or two hours about him, and he said, 'Commissioner, I can't do this unless I am assured of your full support.' "

LEDFORD: The ball was now back in Happy's court. He had to make a play. His decision would either go unnoticed, or it would make him awfully unpopular. It might even cost him his job. So what did Happy tell Rickey?

CHANDLER: "I said to him, 'Branch, I'm gonna have to meet my Maker some day, and if he asks me why I didn't let this boy play, even though he has talent, and I can think of a number, Josh Gibson and Buck Leonard and those fellas with great talent who never got to play.' And I said to Branch, 'If he asks me, my Maker, why I didn't let this boy play, and I say it's because he's black, it might not be a satisfactory answer.' I said, 'You bring him in, and we'll make the fight with you, and it'll be 15-2. I'll approve the transfer of his contract from Montreal to Brooklyn.' If Landis had been Commissioner, Robinson couldn't have played. I know I was more responsible for it than anybody on earth, you understand."

LEDFORD: Happy Chandler's monumental decision transcended the sport of baseball. It was much more than just a decision to integrate a single sport. It was, in every way, one of the most important decisions in the history of our society.

COACH CHANDLER

(While all Kentuckians are familiar with Happy Chandler's record as governor, senator and baseball commissioner, few are aware of his record as a football coach.)

LEDFORD: Happy Chandler found his greatest success in politics and baseball, but as a young man, Happy was an outstanding athlete. He played several sports at Transylvania, and when he graduated, his ambition was to become a football coach.

CHANDLER: "I had gone to Versailles in 1922, and I coached the football team over there eight years. We won 36 games, lost 15 and tied 5. So I had a pretty good football coaching record. I coached the freshman team in 1927 over at Danville. I also did some scouting during this 10-year period. Even after I was elected Lieutenant Governor, I continued to do some scouting for them. I had developed a knack for observing the other team's play, and I did pretty well at it."

LEDFORD: Chandler moved out of the high school ranks as an assistant coach at Centre College. Centre had the area's most powerful football program in those days. Happy was the coach of the freshman team. His young Praying Colonels were undefeated going into the final game against Kentucky Wesleyan. Centre's head coach had already announced his resignation, and Happy felt if he could win that final game, he would have a great shot at the top job.

CHANDLER: "Dick Gallagher, who later got to be the head of the Football Hall of Fame, was a quarterback for Kentucky Wesleyan. I had them beaten all day, 6-0. I was directly responsible for them, this is 1927, with the clock going up to 20 seconds until the finish. I can still see him. He faded back in midfield and threw a long pass. I thought the fella caught it in Garrard County, but they said he caught it behind the goal line. They kicked the point after the game was over and beat me 7-6. When I lost that game at Centre over there, 7 to 6, I went around to every convenient brick wall I could find, trying to butt my brains out. You know, because it happened so suddenly and with no time left, you understand?"

LEDFORD: Centre passed over Happy as the head coach but wanted him to come back again the next season as an assistant. He made the decision to get out of coaching and get on with his life. That led to him twice being Governor of Kentucky, serving the state as a U.S. Senator, and later being named Commissioner of baseball. His tremendous career of service might not have been possible had if not been for a freshman quarterback from Kentucky Wesleyan.

CHANDLER: "Ever since then, every year at Christmas time, including the year just past, I get a letter from Gallagher, saying, 'Dear Happy, remember me, I'm the fella that made a Governor out of you.'

LEDFORD: Dick Gallagher, we all owe you a debt of thanks. That touchdown pass of yours took Happy Chandler away from Centre College and gave him to the state of Kentucky.

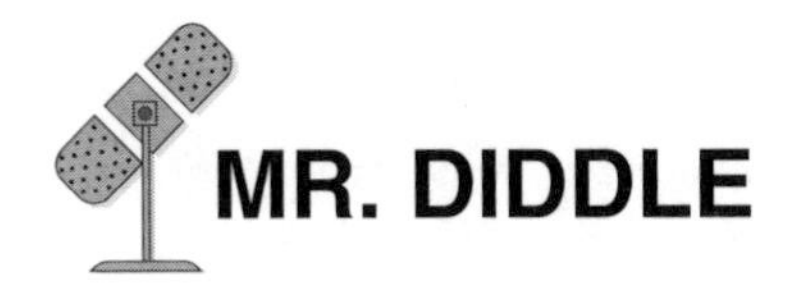

MR. DIDDLE

(In all of college basketball history, the fourth winningest coach is Edgar Allen Diddle. The big four are Adolph Rupp, Phog Allen, Henry Iba and Diddle, who fashioned his great winning record at Western Kentucky University.)

LEDFORD: Ed Diddle was born on a farm outside Gradyville, Ky. He was such an outstanding basketball player at the old Columbia High School in Adair County that Centre College, one of the most powerful athletic schools in the area at that time, won him over. Centre was becoming a national football power in those long ago days, and the college wasn't about to miss out on a good athlete.

DIDDLE: "Yes, I went to Centre as a basketball player. In fact, I had never seen a football game when I entered Centre College. The first game I ever saw, I played in."

LEDFORD: What Ed Diddle was to learn in the first game he played in was that clipping was legal. And he found out the hard way. In a game against Tennessee in Knoxville, he was repeatedly leveled by those blocks from behind.

DIDDLE: "They clipped me so many times that I got so that when the ball would get up to within three or four feet of them, I'd just lay down. Uncle Charlie Moran, my coach, and Chief Myers called me up to the sideline and wanted to know what I was laying down for. I told them that was better than getting hurt, and that I'd be able to play next week."

LEDFORD: Well, Ed Diddle became a good football player, but after leaving Centre College, it was his first love — basketball — that led him to a great career.

DIDDLE: "I had always wanted to coach. It was my sole ambition to coach, so I went to Monticello, Kentucky. That was February 1920. I took that fine team to the state tournament at Lexington, and there I was defeated by Louisville Manuel 20 to 19."

LEDFORD: Although his first team came within one point of winning the state championship, Mr. Diddle would later say that the coaching profession almost got the best of him those first six or seven years.

DIDDLE: "I couldn't eat, I couldn't sleep, I couldn't coach."

LEDFORD: I don't know about his lack of appetite or his insomnia, but Ed Diddle could always coach. He went on to success at Greenville High School, then, in 1922, he became the third coach in Western's history. He remained at Western for his entire college career, a career that spanned 42 years. At Western, Mr. Diddle's trademark became the red towel. It began at Tennessee Tech one night with Western trailing by one point. Carl Lamarr fired up the game's last shot, a long two-handed set shot that was on target.

DIDDLE: "When he did that, that made us win the game. I took the old towel, which was wet as water, and threw it up over my head and hit the ceiling of the gym. Well, it came back down all over my head. I looked like an Indian squaw with that towel over my head. The boys got a big kick out of it."

LEDFORD: Everybody got a big kick out of it...and the towel and Ed Diddle became synonymous. At Tennessee Tech, the towel was white. That soon changed, however.

DIDDLE: "I went to the red towel because our colors here at the college were red. And I remember a company sending me a whole crate of towels...of red towels. And every Christmas I have received thousand of red ties and red towels."

LEDFORD: The first basketball arena in Kentucky to honor a basketball coach was built on the Western campus...the E.A. Diddle Arena. And to this day, when the Hilltoppers are on the run, the red towels are waving. That continuing tradition is a tribute to the great coach Ed Diddle.

Western Kentucky's E.A. Diddle Arena is named in honor of the fourth-winningest coach in all of collegiate basketball.

THE GOLDEN BOY

(One of the greatest football players ever from the state of Kentucky was Paul Hornung. The former "Golden Boy" was an all-state selection, a Heisman Trophy winner and an All-Pro with the Green Bay Packers. He is also a member of the NFL Hall of Fame.)

LEDFORD: Louisville native Paul Hornung began his football career at Flaget High School. After gaining All-American status at Flaget, Hornung had to make a tough decision on where to attend college. He had one school in mind, but his mother thought otherwise.

HORNUNG: "I wanted to go to UK, actually. Bear Bryant was the head coach there at the time and I was really leaning toward Kentucky. My mother wanted me to go to Notre Dame. Although she left the choice up to me, in those days, your mother usually makes the choice."

LEDFORD: Even though Hornung was impressed by Bear Bryant and the UK program, it was his mother and a former high school teammate who ultimately influenced his decision.

HORNUNG: "When I went to Notre Dame, when I made my only visit to Notre Dame, Sherrill Sipes, who was an all-state halfback here with me in Louisville at Flaget, really wanted to go to Notre Dame. So it was kind of like he and I decided we wanted to go to the same school together. He and my mother won out, I guess."

LEDFORD: After winning the Heisman Trophy at Notre Dame, Hornung was drafted into the NFL by the Green Bay Packers. His coach was the legendary Vince Lombardi. Lombardi had the reputation of being a brutal taskmaster, but Hornung says his relationship with his coach was ideal.

HORNUNG: "Well, I don't know, I related very well to the coach. And I did something that none of the other players could probably do at that time. He could get on my butt, and he really could. I was his whipping boy, but he knew that it wouldn't affect me mentally. There were some other football players that we had that were great football players, but he knew if he could, when I made a mistake, if he could get on my butt and push me and holler at me and discipline me, he knew that he could discipline every other football player on the team."

LEDFORD: Hornung's career in the NFL spanned nine seasons. As one of the game's premier running backs, he was the target of every mean-spirited and unhappy defender. He faced them all, but for Hornung, there is one defender who stands out as the toughest he ever faced.

HORNUNG: "Well, Dick Butkus was the best football player that I've ever played against, period. I always felt that Johnny Unitas was the best quarterback that I'd ever seen at that time, but Butkus, to me, was absolutely the most demanding football player I've ever played against. He was the prototype of all middle linebackers, and we had a great one playing with us, Ray Nitschke. I mean, both those kids from the University of Illinois, you know. How do you rank them, both of them in the top five linebackers of all-time. But Butkus, to me, was the most intimidating football player I'd ever seen. He hated everybody. He'd hate his mother if she was out on the field."

LEDFORD: Hornung is now living and working in Louisville. He's also hosting the Paul Hornung Sports Showcase, a weekly sports show that can be seen nationwide on SportsChannel. But for those of us who remember him, indeed, for all football fans, Paul Hornung will always be remembered as "The Golden Boy" on those great Packer teams of the 1960s.

MASTER TEACHER

(Bobby Knight may be a controversial and enigmatic man, but when it comes to coaching the game of basketball, no one does it better. During his illustrious career, Knight has led Indiana to three NCAA championships. He has also coached gold medal winning U.S. teams in the Olympics and the Pan American Games.)

LEDFORD: During the Final Four in Denver, *The Denver Post* conducted a poll among 100 Division I coaches, asking them to name the best X's and O's coach. The group selected Indiana's Bob Knight. It's difficult to argue with that selection. His teams have captured three NCAA championships and one NIT title. In addition, he coached American teams to an Olympic gold medal and a Pan American gold medal. What's the secret to Knight's success? Perhaps it's because Knight likes to think of himself as a teacher and educator.

KNIGHT: "I simply try to teach by breaking it down into small parts, going through those parts with you as a player. I think it's more important that you understand what basketball is all about, that you understand what to look for. What to anticipate. Then what kind of skills you have. And I use a little analogy for our players. Sherlock Holmes once told Dr. Watson, `Watson, all see, but few perceive.' So I kind of paraphrase that a little bit, and I say, 'Hey, every player looks, but there aren't very many of them that see.' "

LEDFORD: Knight has been Big Ten Coach of the Year six times, National Coach of the Year three times. In coaching, Knight puts great emphasis on anticipation, on teaching his players to anticipate what may happen, especially while they're playing defense.

KNIGHT: "What I need to do with you is show you that in this given position, defensively, where you happen to be, with the ball in this position, there are only two or three things that can happen. Now, once we teach you that, then you can learn to anticipate those one or two or three things that might happen. Given these circumstances, the ball here...you here...your man here."

LEDFORD: Knight's teams have always been known for their tenacious defense. Also, for being intelligent. He believes if he can recruit top athletes and make them smart basketball players, his teams will always be competitive.

KNIGHT: "You can get players to play better. I really believe that in getting players to play better, the first thing is to get them to think better. I believe concentration is the key through which player development occurs. And the player that concentrates best is going to be the best basketball player, and the player with the most talent who concentrates best is going to be a truly great player."

LEDFORD: Bobby Knight has earned the respect of his coaching peers. According to them, he's the best. And judging from Knight's outstanding record, it's hard to argue otherwise.

LIVING LEGEND

(One of the true legends of college football is here in the Bluegrass State. His name...Roy Kidd. Coach Kidd has been at Eastern Kentucky University for 26 seasons, during which he has built the Colonels into a national power.)

LEDFORD: Roy Kidd grew up in the southeastern Kentucky town of Corbin. He made all-state in basketball, baseball and football as a Redhound. His success continued to grow as Kidd was named an All-American quarterback his senior year at Eastern Kentucky University. After graduating, Kidd turned Richmond's Madison High into a state power, recording a 54-10 record in just six seasons. In 1964, Kidd took over the reigns at his alma mater, and it's there he has recorded 208 victories. Where does his success lie?

KIDD: "Like any coach, I think you've got to have good players. And I think I've been very fortunate to have good players. My coaching staff has pretty well stayed with me intact, although we have lost a coach here and there. I think that's very important...if you can keep your coaches and do a good job recruiting. I think any coach is just as good as his players."

LEDFORD: And his players have been dynamite. They've led the Colonels to the NCAA Division I-AA playoffs 10 of the last 11 years. Included in that string are four-straight appearances in the NCAA Championship game, in which the Colonels brought home the big trophy in 1979 and 1982. The key to Kidd's success lies in his attitude toward recruiting. Although he coaches at the Division I-AA level, he doesn't back away from the Division I prospects.

KIDD: "If I go out and do like you said and try to recruit a

I-AA football player, I'm not going to win. So I go out and recruit a I-A player and he's just going to play in a I-AA league, so to say. But that's what we recruit. We recruit kids that we think can win at a I-A level."

LEDFORD: And won they have. During the decade of the '80s, EKU has recorded more victories than any other I-AA school. And they're third nationally in wins behind only Nebraska and Brigham Young. However, with all the success Kidd has had, he wishes he could change one major area of the program...keeping his coaches from teaching classes."

KIDD: "My coaches teach anywhere from four to five classes. It's almost like on a high school level. I don't see how they do it."

LEDFORD: But for now, as the 1990 season approaches, Kidd looks to improve on last year's 9-3 playoff team. He returns an unbelievable backfield anchored by a four-year starter...quarterback Lorenzo Fields. Fields, along with running backs Tim Lester and Marcus Thomas, should lead the Colonels well into the playoffs. But for that to happen, Kidd says improvement is vital.

KIDD: "I think the team, what we've got to do this year is develop more togetherness. I do not feel like we were together last year. I thought we had a little more individualism on our team. You're not going to win that way; you've got to win together with everybody working together. I emphasized that all spring to our players, and that's the thing. I know we've got experience and we've got a lot of lettermen, and I know we've got a lot of good players, but we've got to get that chemistry to put it all together."

LEDFORD: With Roy Kidd as the teacher, look for team chemistry to be an easy subject. And watch for the Colonels to take their success into the '90s.

CLEM "THE GEM"

(Clem Haskins earned All-American honors at Western Kentucky University. He later became the head coach at WKU, before moving on to take the Minnesota job. Haskins, however, came close to being a Louisville Cardinal rather than a Hilltopper.)

LEDFORD: Being a first is nothing new for Clem Haskins. He was the first black to integrate into the Taylor County school system from the old Campbellsville Durham High. He was among the first blacks to play at Western, and he later became the first black coach at that school. As a prep player, Haskins could do it all...run, jump, shoot and play defense. In 1963, Haskins signed to play college ball...not with Western Kentucky where he became an All-American, but with the University of Louisville.

HASKINS: "I had really made a decision to go to Western all along, but it was kind of a last minute decision to go to Louisville. I changed my mind in the summer. I entered Western Kentucky late in the fall. I loved Western. I loved it on day one. A lot of time in recruiting things happen...young people get twisted, and I got twisted and signed for the wrong reason. I'm happy today to be a Western Kentucky graduate. I went there and enjoyed four years and had a great time."

LEDFORD: Clem has many memories from his playing days at Western. One came from the 1966 NCAA tournament. Oddly enough, it's a memory of a game that was never played.

HASKINS: "Getting to the second round in 1966 was a big highlight. We played Michigan and they beat us on a jump ball. It was a tough call. The next night we'd have played the great Kentucky ballclub. So I think that's one of the great games that's perhaps never taken place. That was two outstanding teams. We were similar, so it was gonna be one of the greatest games ever played in the state. I would say that's one of the highlights that never happened."

LEDFORD: However, Clem says the fondest memory from his basketball career was playing in the high school Sweet 16 tournament. He says that memory stands head and shoulders above the rest.

HASKINS: "I've had many great moments as a high school player, college player, pro player and in coaching, but I think playing in the Sweet 16 here in Louisville's Freedom Hall in 1963 was perhaps the highlight of my career. We played before 16,000 fans, and for a little country boy coming into a place like that, I'll never forget it. My father walked in and said, 'My God, if we could fill this with hay, we'd have enough hay to last us the rest of our lives.' "

LEDFORD: Clem Haskins has come a long way since his Taylor County days. After playing in the NBA for nine years, Haskins took the head coaching job at his alma mater in Bowling Green in 1980. Six years later, he moved on to Minnesota, where in 1990, he led the Golden Gophers to the NCAA Final Eight.

HASKINS: "We had two difficult years, rebuilding our program. We only won nine ballgames, 10 games. Of course, the last two years, we get to the Sweet 16 one year and then last year to the final eight. We were only 80 minutes away from being the national champs, so I would have to say to you it's been a great four years at Minnesota and I look forward to seeing that many more years."

LEDFORD: When Clem Haskins is not coaching or recruiting, the 47-year-old father of two can be found farming 500 acres. He does it because he never forgot where he came from or the hard work that got him to the top.

THE OTHER CHAMP

(Louisville has always been known as the home of boxing great Muhammad Ali. But another boxer from that city also won the WBA heavyweight title in 1968. His name was Jimmy Ellis.)

LEDFORD: Jimmy Ellis began his boxing career while still a youngster at the old Ferguson Youth Center in Louisville. His professional career included 53 matches. His final record was 40-12-1. Included among his wins were 24 knockouts. During his career, Ellis fought many of the best fighters of that era, but in his mind, there's no question who was the best...his hometown rival, Muhammad Ali.

ELLIS: "What made Ali so great was that he was able to get off the floor, come back and finish you off. If the fight was really close, he was able to pick it up in the later rounds and pick you off. I saw him call rounds when we were amateurs, and say you're going in two, and the guy'd go in two. He'd say he'd go in three, he'd go in three. There were different things that he did that made him so great."

LEDFORD: Yes, to many, Muhammad Ali was the greatest fighter of all time. And Ellis should know. He fought Ali several times in the amateur ranks before meeting him professionally in Houston in 1971. It took Ali 12 rounds against Ellis before he earned a knockout. But to Ellis, Ali wasn't the toughest puncher he had faced. That honor went to Ernie Shavers. Ellis fought "The Acorn" in New York at the newly remodeled Madison Square Garden. Ellis wanted to take Shavers out early, but Shavers had a different script in mind, a script that put Ellis down for the count.

ELLIS: "I thought the referee was cheating me, because the guy hit me with a shot. I had him in trouble, then the guy hit me with a shot and all I could hear was, six, seven, eight. I thought the referee's got to be cheating because he started at six. But while all that was going on, before I opened my eyes, I heard the guy say six. When I opened my eyes, Madison Square Garden looked like a spaceship to me because it had all these arms and lights and I thought I was on a spaceship."

LEDFORD: The spaceship took off and left Ellis behind. He was counted out by the referee. But Ellis didn't lose very often. He won the WBA heavyweight championship in 1968 with a victory over Jerry Quarry. He also defended his title successfully against Floyd Patterson. Ellis then retired in 1975, and unlike other retired fighters, he has never returned to the ring. One fighter who has is George Foreman, and Ellis warns that you shouldn't underestimate the over-40 fighter.

ELLIS: "Everybody is talking about, he's old, he's old and he is up in age, but Foreman's got a lot of punching power. If you underestimate him, you're gonna get beat because he will stand there — he's got a good defense — and he will get you outta there."

LEDFORD: Ellis says he looks forward to seeing Foreman in the ring with "Iron" Mike Tyson. Ellis feels it should be an interesting contest. As for Jimmy Ellis, he hasn't seen any more spaceships for awhile. Currently, he is a member of the Kentucky Hall of Fame and spends most of his time watching his 6-5, 265-pound son, Jeff, play tight end for Ohio State. With that size, his son could probably outbox his father...but I doubt it.

BEST SEAT IN THE HOUSE

(Lexington native Doug Flynn was a member of those Big Red Machine powerhouses in Cincinnati back in the mid-1970s. As a member of the Reds, Flynn earned himself a reputation as a solid defensive player. He also earned a pair of World Series rings.)

LEDFORD: October is a baseball player's favorite month. Time for the big show — the World Series — to have its big dance. Former Cincinnati Red Doug Flynn recalls his World Series days. In 1975 and 1976, Flynn played on two World Series teams for the Reds. They won both series...4-3 against Boston in '75 and 4-0 against the New York Yankees in '76.

FLYNN: "When I look back on it now, I can say I was in two World Series. Well, I had great seats but I didn't get to play."

LEDFORD: Doug never saw action on the field in either series. He backed up Pete Rose at third base throughout both seasons, yet even in 1976, with the Reds up three games to none, manager Sparky Anderson elected to stay with the starters. Doug says playing the waiting game was tough.

FLYNN: "There was a lot of pressure even if you weren't playing in it. I think there was less pressure if you were playing. Because if you weren't, you were sitting there thinking about it. I'm 24-years old in the first one and I'm sitting there thinking, 'Let's see, I'm making a salary of $16,500. If we win the World Series, I'm gonna make another $14,000. Good Lord, this is $30,000, this is more money than I know what to do with.' So those thoughts were going through your mind, but you were thinking, 'Man, I get to wear that big ring around all the time and that'll be neat, and we'll be world champions.' And there were a lot of flash-backs. You know, I couldn't even make it in college, but here's an opportunity now to be on a championship ballclub."

LEDFORD: In what was one of the most memorable World Series of all time — the '75 matchup with the Red Sox — Flynn sat through several days of rain in Boston. It was a wait he wasn't prepared for.

FLYNN: "Here we are with three sets of clothes for a week trip. We're washing stuff out in the sink, and sending stuff out to dry cleaners. Well, I didn't have money for dry cleaners. We ended up borrowing money from some of the veterans that were there. And, of course, they'd go out and buy new stuff, while we're sitting there wondering how in the world can I wash out my underwear and my shirt to wear for the next day. So you spent most of the day just hanging around the hotel because you didn't have anything to wear out."

LEDFORD: Oh, how salaries have changed since Doug played for Cincy. But one thing that remains are the memories. Of course, when people remember that game, they invariably remember the dramatic 12th inning home run Red Sox catcher Carlton Fisk hit to give Boston a 7-6 victory and force a seventh game. It was a classic. Flynn recalls a question that one reporter asked Pete Rose after the game.

FLYNN: "This reporter says, 'Pete, you guys have to feel like you're in trouble now. I mean, you just got beat in a game that you had the lead. Now you're going to the seventh game. How do you feel?' Pete says, 'How do I feel? It's the greatest game ever, and I was a part of it. Tomorrow we're going with our ace. Don Gullett's gonna be on the mound in the seventh game of the World Series. I think we've got to feel pretty good about it.' Sure enough, we went out and won."

LEDFORD: Doug, you've got to feel pretty good too. You were a vital part of the Big Red Machine that won two championships. And even though you didn't play, you had a great seat..right in the front row.

THE FIRST LADY OF COLLEGE HOOPS

(Kentucky Coach Rick Pitino made history in the summer of 1990 when he hired the first woman basketball coach for a Division I men's team. The bright and intelligent young lady who broke new ground was former Georgia Lady Bulldog Bernadette Locke.)

LEDFORD: On June 13, 1990, Bernadette Locke was thrust into the national spotlight as the first female basketball coach for a Division I men's team. Locke is a 1981 graduate of the University of Georgia and was an All-American guard for the Lady Bulldogs. After seven years as an assistant coach at Georgia, she says she felt ready for the challenge Kentucky offered.

LOCKE: "Coach Pitino and I talked about that and, being single, not having any children and the age that I was, the young age that I am, I could take the challenge, and take the chance, and that's what I want. I want to look at myself three years from now, where I want to be, the things I want to achieve, and it was a great opportunity for me."

LEDFORD: Some skeptics accused Pitino of hiring a woman strictly for publicity purposes. As things turned out, the skeptics were proved wrong. Pitino had specific duties outlined for Coach Locke, which included on-the-floor coaching, on-campus recruiting, and working as a liaison between the basketball staff and the academic staff.

LOCKE: "My main responsibility is going to be career placement for our players, which is a great credit to Coach Pitino for bringing it about for them."

LEDFORD: When Pitino arrived at Kentucky, he was skeptical about the passion for Kentucky basketball that existed throughout the Bluegrass state. That changed in a hurry. It didn't take long before Pitino understood how fanatical Kentucky fans can be. So how did he explain it to Bernadette?

LOCKE: "When he was describing to me the passion here, it actually floored me. I was talking to Coach Newton, and he said, 'You know, you're familiar with Georgia football, right?' I said I was. He said, 'Now magnify that.' It was, like, beyond disbelief. He said, 'That's the people of Kentucky, the state of Kentucky, that's their love of basketball here, and it's just a phenomenon.' And he was right."

LEDFORD: When Bernadette came to UK, she was immediately thrust into the role of pioneer in an all male-dominated field. That's a label she can live without.

LOCKE: "I don't want to be labeled as a woman's coach in a men's sector. For so many years, men have been involved in women's sports, so I see it as only fitting for women to be involved in men's sports."

NOW, THAT'S A LOSS

(On Oct. 7, 1916, Georgia Tech met Cumberland College of Lebanon, Tennessee in Atlanta. The game turned out to be the biggest mismatch in college football history.)

LEDFORD: At the time, John "The Wizard" Heisman was building a national football power at Georgia Tech. His team wasn't expecting much trouble from Cumberland College. But just winning wasn't enough for Heisman. According to Furman Bisher, the sports editor of *The Atlanta Journal*, the size of the win was important to Heisman.

BISHER: "John Heisman had decided that the way to make an impression around the United States was to run up a big score. He felt people noticed that. And that the bigger the score you ran up, the more attention you got. So he decided when they were playing this little helpless team from Cumberland College that he was going to try to see how many points a team of his could actually score in a football game."

LEDFORD: Heisman had offered Cumberland the then-astronomical sum of $500 to come to Atlanta to play. Cumberland, like any good fish, took the bait.

BISHER: "Cumberland was not a very organized football program. Some of the kids were actually members of the football team. But they had to augment the squad by going around the campus and getting volunteers to go down with the team. Some of them went because they just wanted to see Atlanta. They'd never been to a big city before."

LEDFORD: On the pullman ride from Lebanon, the 16-man squad stopped off in Nashville, hoping to recruit some Vanderbilt players to take along. Not only were there no takers, three of the Cumberland players got off the train. George Howard was a campus stringer at the game for *The Atlanta Journal.* He remembers the game well.

HOWARD: "This kid was supposed to walk up and down the sidelines on the telephone and give them a play-by-play back to the office, where some fellow was sitting down there typing the play-by-play. Well, every time Georgia Tech would get the football, this kid would say, 'Uh, Judy Harlan ran for a touchdown' or somebody else ran for a touchdown. And, finally, the fellow at the desk said, 'Kid, you've got this all wrong. You know anything about football?' And the kid said, 'Yes, sir. I sure do. I've been seeing football all my life.' "

LEDFORD: The man on *The Atlanta Journal* desk couldn't believe the reports, so he quickly dispatched a reporter to the stadium.

HOWARD: "They'd sent this fellow out there to double check on it because they knew the kid didn't know what he was doing. But they were wrong, because what they found out confirmed that he was correct, that, indeed, he was giving the correct report back to *The Atlanta Journal* office. First, it was 55-0, then 90-0, then 160-0. He was giving them the factual report."

LEDFORD: Everytime Georgia Tech got the football, six more points went up on the scoreboard. Things were going horribly for Cumberland.

HOWARD: "Cumberland backed up all day long. I don't think they moved forward a yard."

LEDFORD: When it was over, when the game mercifully ended, Cumberland had minus 45 yards. Georgia Tech did not throw a pass, yet racked up 978 yards and 32 touchdowns. Tech had beaten Cumberland College 220-0. Furman

Bisher says there's another interesting statistic to that game.

BISHER: "The game was never played out in its entirety. It was shortened by 12 minutes."

LEDFORD: Someday, somewhere, when a team has been beaten badly on a Saturday afternoon, maybe the coach will gather his players around and tell them the story of little Cumberland College...and that 220-0 loss to Georgia Tech. That's bound to make them feel better.

CAWOOD'S
COMMENTS

WE SAY EITHER, THEY SAY EYE-THER 6/29/79

Surely my ears had deceived me. When driving alone, I always search my radio dial for sports scores. While driving down Highway 25, deep into the mountains, I was able to tune in on a sports program. The reporter had an Eastern Kentucky accent, but that's no problem with me. I speak that accent fluently, having grown up in the area. He was articulate and knowledgeable in reporting the scores. But when he laid an "eye-ther" on me, I almost wrecked the car. That pronunciation of either just doesn't fit with a mountain accent. I can handle it OK if I'm conversing with a New Yorker or somebody from up East. But to me the pronunciation "eye-ther" in our part of the world sounds phoney and highfalutin'. But you know, when I got back to Lexington I noticed something. I noticed a whole bunch of people in my profession of radio and TV have fallen in love with the pronunciation "eye-ther." That doesn't fit any better in the Bluegrass than it does in the mountains.

I've studied on this for several days now and I've come up with my own theory. I believe that Walter Cronkite is the culprit. I caught him saying "eye-ther" on one of his reports. Now, Uncle Walter's roots are in the southwest, but I suppose he was a correspondent in England long enough to change the way he pronounces the word.

But we're not in England, we're in Kentucky. Will you do this for me? The next time you go to a party or a social gathering and you overhear someone use the word "eye-ther," will you walk up to that person and ask if they are from out of state or on radio or TV. I sincerely believe that the answer will be "yes" to one of your questions. I don't know a native Kentuckian not on radio or TV who says "eye-ther." Do you? My dictionary tells me that either...or eye-ther...is correct. But while in Kentucky, let's speak like the rest of our neighbors. We'll say either and let them say "eye-ther."

DEAR WILDCAT FAN 9/1/80

You are the most unique person I have ever known. Each autumn, Saturday after Saturday, you make your way to Lexington from all over the state to the football games. Why? I've asked myself that question a hundred times.

You haven't had a lot to cheer about on most of those Saturdays. I can understand the fan enthusiasm at schools like Alabama and Georgia, but your devotion to UK football is, as the King of Siam said, "a puzzlement." The University brass felt like Kentucky's program had to improve when the Wildcats moved to Commonwealth Stadium if they were going to be able to pay off the mortgage. They needn't have worried. You've filled those 58,000 seats almost every game. Almost every season is a sellout.

Kentucky's program has improved since the move from old Stoll Field, yet going into this season, the Cats were playing only a little better than .500 ball...41 wins, 37 losses and one tie. Still, you pack the place.

Coach Fran Curci, in his speeches around the state, likes to compare the Kentucky program to those at Arkansas and Nebraska. His contention is that, like the other two, Kentucky is a state that is basically interested in one team. He's right. You have given the Wildcats your total support. You come from every nook and cranny of this state. But that doesn't completely explain it either. Arkansas and Nebraska have powerful football programs. In most seasons, both will be ranked among the nation's major powers. It's easy for them to get state-wide support. So that's not the total answer.

I confess I don't know what makes you tick. I don't quite understand the overwhelming support you give the Kentucky football program. I do know this: the University is mighty lucky to have you.

CHOKING 1/4/83

If you want to lay a supreme insult on a coach, a player, an official or anyone connected with a sport, just accuse that person of choking.

In case you haven't been to a game in the past 10 years, choking means a person in the heat of battle, under all kinds of pressure, can't perform up to his potential. He chokes. A couple of men have written a book called "Don't Choke." They say anxiety is the most important opponent a player has to face to overcome the tendency to choke. The authors contend that choking is mental, and one of the best ways to combat it is to use visual imagery. The men write, "See yourself as a winner...and see yourself doing the things that make you a winner."

That's the same message Jerry Claiborne preached to the Kentucky football team last season. He gave each player a copy of the book "Psycho-Cybernetics." In that book, Dr. Malz stresses visualization — seeing yourself as a winner.

Choke is a horrible word to say around people in sports. If you don't believe me, just go up to somebody and grab your throat with one hand. Don't even say the word "choke." They'll get the message. But when they do, get ready to defend yourself.

TV'S INFLUENCE 1/10/83

Soon, the courts will decide if the NCAA will continue to control the TV rights to college football, or if each school is free to make its own deal.

First, here's a little background. A Denver judge, ruling in a case brought by the Universities of Georgia and Oklahoma, declared that the colleges did have the right to make their own deals. That ruling is being appealed. If it's upheld, college football will never be the same again. The big-name schools will be on TV all the time. Teams like Notre Dame would benefit the most. Then the top teams near the large markets would be next in line.

In the long run, it's going to cost most of the schools money. Before a stay of the ruling was put into effect, Oklahoma and Georgia were able to put their games up for bids. The top buck was $250,000. A hundred stations agreed to tie into the network. The $250,000 is nothing to sneeze at, but it's peanuts compared to what the networks are already paying.

The colleges — those that are marketable for television — think there's big money in cable TV. Down the road there might be, but not right now. College basketball, which is not restricted by the NCAA, has found that out. The schools are almost giving away their rights to cable networks. The bottom line is that college basketball is in grave danger of being overexposed.

In the final analysis, I hope the NCAA wins for the good of the game, as well as the good of college football.

HIGH-SCORING LOSERS 3/1/83

It's certainly no secret. Every basketball player I ever met likes to score and score a lot. But have you noticed that teams with the super scorers seldom win championships?

As I checked out the latest national college statistics the other day, I noticed some of the top-ranked teams in the country have players ranked near the top in rebounding, free throw shooting and field goal percentage. The one thing the top teams all had in common is that none had a player at the top of the individual scoring category.

I had to run my finger way down the list to find a player from one of the top-ranked teams. The first one I came upon was Sidney Green of UNLV, and he only ranks 23rd on the list. The next stop is way down at number 50, Steve Stipanovich of Missouri. So the proof's in the pudding. But you can't blame the players for wanting to have gaudy scoring averages. After all, the fans love to see them.

While Pete Maravich was at LSU, he led the nation in scoring and, in the process, drew huge crowds to every gym in the Southeastern Conference. But while Pete scored, LSU lost.

I think about those corny signs coaches put up on the locker room walls. The most popular one reads, "There is no 'I' in team." In college basketball, it seems to be true.

THE MORGAN 5/25/83

Our country is more than 200 years old. It's amazing to me how few animals — breeds of animals — this country has produced. Almost all breeds of cattle have foreign origins. As far as I know, the Boston Terrier is the only breed of dog that was produced in the United States.

The one animal that is the exception is the horse and the United States has produced several breeds. This area of the U.S. is closely associated with the thoroughbred. Well, forget it. He's as English as kidney-pie. However, there is one breed we can call our own and it was developed right here in the state of Kentucky — the American Saddlebred. But the Saddlebred is not the most unusual horse developed in the U.S. That distinction belongs to the Morgan, which was developed in New England. Every registered Morgan can be traced to one horse, and that's unusual. He was a sturdy little sire named Figure who was owned by a Vermont school teacher named Justin Morgan. Figure's name was later changed to that of his owner. As far as I know, the Morgan is the only breed of horse that can be traced to one foundation stallion. The Morgan is a very versatile horse and it exhibits that versatility at the Morgan shows.

A "REAL" SPRING GAME 6/3/83

What is so rare as a day in June?

How about a day in June where a college football coach doesn't come out in favor of playing a real spring game. If it didn't happen, that would be rare. Now I'm not talking about the intrasquad scrimmages most of us have become accustomed to. I'm talking about a real football game with an actual opponent.

This year, Georgia coach Vince Dooley voiced his opinion in favor of such a contest. He joins a long list of college coaches who have proclaimed the same over the past few years.

Their arguments are sensible. The players would put a lot more into spring practice if they knew they were going to face a "real" opponent at the end of the spring session. The game would generate real income, which makes the proposal more enticing to administrators, since nearly every college in the country is having financial problems these days.

The game wouldn't count in the standings for the fall, but wouldn't it be interesting to see a Kentucky-Louisville game at the end of spring practice? Or how about UK-Eastern, or a UK-West Virginia game? It does sound exciting.

Under present NCAA rules, colleges can't play an outside opponent in the spring. Maybe it's against the rules because it makes too much sense. That's probably why they've never tried it.

FEARLESS 7/12/83

Everyone of us has experienced fear — raw, stark fear. It's one of the most unpleasant emotions known to man. I got to thinking about how some athletes must deal with their fear.

Football, basketball and baseball players must experience it. So must every other athlete. But I think the solo players, those that aren't members of a team, must bare the heaviest burden.

Chris Lewis must have felt fear as a virtual unknown tennis player on Centre Court of the famed Wimbledon tournament, facing John McEnroe, one of the greatest players in the world.

It must also be agonizing, the fear the matador feels before going into the ring with a bull. I think the jockeys who ride in the Kentucky Derby must experience fear. All the hoopla, the large fields, a certain amount of danger to man and beast all contribute to fear. I think it's the main reason some of the best jockeys in the sport have ridden poorly in the Derby. A man's judgment comes into question when he experiences fear.

Those of us who have never been in that type of situation can't possibly know what the athlete feels. All of us, athletes included, operate at a much higher level when we experience a feeling of confidence. Confidence and fear are never present at the same time.

We may not have ridden in a Kentucky Derby, been in a ring with an angry bull, but we have, all of us, experienced fear.

I thought about this the other day while I was sitting in the dentist's chair.

THE QUOTABLE ABE 12/6/83

I guess it's been 10 years now. That's when I first heard Abe Lemons speak. He slouched all over the speaker's stand, fondling an unlit cigar, but in a matter of minutes he had his audience laughing in the aisles.

Abe was the basketball coach then at Oklahoma City. He has since moved on to Pan American, and to Texas, and now he's back at Oklahoma City. An article in a recent issue of The Sporting News came up with some notable quotables from Abe Lemons. After a questionable call, Abe said the official was driving him out of coaching. Lemons said he was going to get a job in a prison. "I'll be the guy," he said, "that drops the poison pellets in the water and asks the guy if he's sorry."

When asked if he was into jogging, Abe responded, "Hell no. If I die, I want to be sick." On his players, Abe says, "I got one player whose sweat is so rare, it'll cure cancer." On the high turnover in the coaching profession, Coach Lemons said, "Some alumni offered to buy up my contract. I told them I didn't have change for a twenty."

Abe says, "We play a sieve zone defense. That's where we leave all five guys wide open. They get so excited, they can't shoot straight."

When he was fired at Texas, Abe was asked if he was bitter toward the school's athletic director, DeLoss Dodds. Abe said he wasn't but then added, "I plan to buy a glass-bottomed car, so I can watch the look on his face when I run him over."

NIGHTMARE IN THE KINGDOME 4/3/84

A strange thing happened to the Kentucky basketball team last Saturday. It choked. The Wildcats lost in their first game in the Final Four to Georgetown 53-40. It was not the loss to a fine Georgetown team that was so painful. It was the way Kentucky lost. Nobody expected it to be a piece of cake against the Hoyas, who went on to win it all, but Kentucky went into the Seattle Kingdome ready to play. With just over three minutes left in the first half, the Cats were on top by 12. A scoring drought set in, yet Kentucky was still in great shape at the intermission with a seven-point advantage.

Who can explain the second half? Not coach Joe B. Hall. Not the players. Sam Bowie said it was sad. That's an understatement. The UK players seemed confused by one of the worst halves of basketball in memory. The Cats fired 21 times at the basket...fired 21 bricks...not a single shot found its mark. It went from bad to worse. For the entire final 20 minutes of the game, Kentucky hit three of 33 shots from the field. No team on earth could have beaten even a weak opponent with such poor marksmanship.

The loss signaled the end for Bowie, Melvin Turpin, Dicky Beal and Jim Master as Kentucky basketball players. Those four seniors can look back over great careers at UK and even an outstanding final season that saw them win 29 games while losing only five. It may take them several years to appreciate their careers at Kentucky, because the Georgetown loss will stick in their craws for a long time.

The fans were disappointed, hoping for one more national title for the Wildcats. But fans bounce back much quicker than the players do. In fact, back at the hotel, one Wildcat fan was busy getting a petition to replay the second half.

JOE B. QUITS 4/1/85

It ended where it began. Right after Kentucky was eliminated in the NCAA tournament last week in Denver, Joe B. Hall announced on his post-game radio program that he was resigning as the head basketball coach. Ironically, it was in the Mile High City that Joe B. got his first head coaching job at Regis College in 1962.

History will be kind to Coach Hall. He fashioned a brilliant 13-year record at UK, yet was never accorded the adulation he deserved. Joe B. had the misfortune of following a legend, replacing Adolph Rupp at UK in 1972. Rupp had been at Kentucky for 42 years and had won more games than any coach in college basketball history. His retirement was forced upon him at the age of 70. It was one of Joe B.'s adversaries, Dale Brown of LSU, who maintained that Hall was the only coach to ever successfully follow a legend. Joe B. never fully escaped the shadow of the man in the brown suit.

But take a look at Hall's record. In 13 years, he led the Wildcats to eight conference championships. His teams made three appearances in the Final Four, winning the NCAA Championship in 1978. His team also won the NIT title in 1976. During his watch at Kentucky, Joe B. produced six All-Americans and nine All-SEC performers.

The bottom line, though, was that Hall took a solid Kentucky program and made it better. I don't think most of us gave him his just due. He toiled for the entire 13 years under the stigma of "Adolph could have done it better." Having been a player at UK and an assistant under Rupp for seven years, he felt the pressure of maintaining the high standards of the program.

He succeeded in spades.

Kentucky fans owe Joe B. Hall their thanks. He has had an outstanding career, and as the years go by, his record will shine brighter and brighter.

GET A BEVO 4/17/87

I've never forgotten the call, it was that unusual. The caller on the other end of the telephone was a young man who had just gotten his first job. He was the sports information director for a small college. He asked my opinion on how he could go about getting some publicity for his school's basketball team. That request was out of my field. "Tell your coach," I told him, "to get himself a Bevo Francis." My young caller had never heard of Bevo Francis. The caller was too young to remember.

But Bevo is the man who put little Rio Grande College on the basketball map. Never before or since has a college basketball player poured points through the hoop like Bevo did. No player has ever averaged more than 45 points a game. No player except Bevo. He played two years at Rio Grande and he filled it up both years. He averaged 46.5 points per game his first year, 48.3 the next. There were no three-point shots in Bevo's day either. He got them the old-fashioned way.

Francis played at Rio Grande during the 1952-53 and '53-54 seasons, and the whole nation followed the progress of that scoring machine.

I don't know whatever happened to Bevo. I guess he never made it in the pros. And we seldom hear anything about Rio Grande College anymore.

My young friend's coach never found a big scorer and that small college is still trying to find a way to get some publicity for its basketball team.

But as the years pass, and the publicity gimmicks come and go, some of us still remember — the best gimmick is a Bevo Francis.

HOLD THE PLAYER RESPONSIBLE

6/1/87

Warner Alford makes sense to me. He's the athletics director at Ole Miss and his football team is serving a two-year probation by the NCAA. The biggest sin committed by Ole Miss was that a coach gave money to a player.

Alford has a refreshing approach to the penalty. He says right up front that Ole Miss deserves the probation. Alford says, "We had a coach break a rule and give a boy money. The boy broke the rule and took the money." Alford points out that while both the coach and the player broke the rules, the coach was fired and the player is still playing.

Mr. Alford recommends that a few more rules are needed, rules that would make the athlete ineligible. Is it fair when a coach is caught cheating he is fired while the athlete goes on playing? Alford says the players know the rules. They know what is legal and what isn't. He thinks the guilty athlete should be ineligible, not every player on the team, as was the case at SMU.

What Warner Alford is saying makes sense. He deserves to be heard. Cheating will never be stamped out as long as the athlete is held blameless. It should carry over into recruiting too. When the colleges decide to put some teeth into the rule, punishing the athlete as well as the coaches and the schools, then, and only then, will there be a chance to clean up college athletics.

KNIGHT 6/8/87

The Supreme Court decision allowing Puerto Rico to extradite a criminal from the United States had hardly been handed down when some crazed maniac was screaming, "Bring back Bobby." No kidding, Puerto Rico wanted to extradite Indiana coach Bob Knight to stand trial for an alleged misdemeanor committed eight years ago. Do you think somebody wanted publicity? You bet! They knew how to get it, too.

Coach Knight was arrested in Puerto Rico in 1979 while coaching the U.S. Basketball team to the Pan American Gold Medal. UK's Kyle Macy was on that team. After he graduated, Kyle wrote a book, and in it he talked about that situation. Macy wrote that the U.S. team still had about 15 minutes left in practice when Brazil's women's team came into the gym. Knight yelled for them to be quiet and that touched off a nerve in a Puerto Rican cop. Macy said it wasn't true that Knight had shouted obscenities. He wrote that an argument ensued, the cop poked coach Knight in the eye, and then took him off to jail in handcuffs.

If Kyle's rendition of what happened is accurate and true, and I believe it is, it will get no further. The Puerto Rico episode has become a nightmare to Knight.

No, it's worse than a nightmare, because even a nightmare will go away — in time.

BIG MAC 7/17/87

The Eastern Kentucky University Alumni Association is going to honor coach Paul McBrayer. On Aug. 3, the alumni are planning a day of golf, and that evening, a banquet for the man who coached the basketball team from 1946 through 1961.

The team was called the Maroons back then, and when a team went into Richmond to play one of Mac's teams, it was always in for a fight. I saw a lot of Eastern's games back in the old Weaver Health Building, and they were, to my way of thinking, the best teams year-after-year that Eastern has turned out.

Mac did it with what he had. He had some excellent basketball players at times, and he had some that weren't exactly blue-chippers. But his teams were always competitive. Combative might be a better choice of words.

Paul was an All-American at the University of Kentucky in 1930, and was an assistant coach at UK until he left for military service during World War II. His job wasn't waiting when he returned, but that was good news for EKU.

If Paul McBrayer had a trademark, it was that his teams played hard, always. Oh, they played better some nights than others, but the players gave it the big effort every game.

When Mac was inducted into the Kentucky Sports Hall of Fame a year ago, his former players came in numbers to honor their old coach. I know of no higher tribute a coach can receive than the honor and respect of the men he led into battle.

OL' JAKE GAITHER 8/12/87

Jake Gaither, an extremely successful football coach at Florida A&M, described what he looked for in a player, "...a-gile, mo-bile and hos-tile." Other coaches loved the quote and it became a part of the college coaching lingo.

Recently, the NCAA interviewed some of the great coaches of the past. Naturally, the former coach of the Rattlers was one of them.

Jake says while he was coaching, his wife, Sadie, was really into the game of football too. She sat high in the stands each Saturday with a pad and pencil in hand. She graded the plays, the players, and even the coaches, especially Jake.

In the interview, he recalled a game when his team was struggling. Up in the stands, a couple of rowdy fans were sitting right behind his wife. They'd had a bit too much of the grape and didn't know Sadie was Jake's wife. Needless to say, they were giving ol' Jake down the road, claiming he couldn't coach, he was too old and that he had no imagination. It was a scoreless game late in the fourth quarter when Florida A&M started a drive. On a pitchout, a Rattler back sprinted all the way down to the 20-yard line. One of the inebriated fans said, "Same play I would have called." On the next play, Florida A&M completed a pass at the five. The man said, "Same play I would have called, exactly." Two plays later A&M had the ball on the one-yard line, third-and-goal. Mrs. Gaither hadn't said a word, but couldn't hold back any longer.

"What play would you call now?" she demanded.

"I got 'em this far," he replied. "Let ol' Jake take 'em in."

Jake Gaither was a great coach with a great sense of humor. They seem to go together, don't they?

WINNING SELLS 8/17/87

There's an old adage in college football that goes, "The offense sells tickets, the defense wins games." That seems contradictory, doesn't it? Would the fans rather see their team score and score and lose, or play it close to the vest and win?

As the late Vince Lombardi taught us, winning is the name of the game and winning will sell tickets.

The late Paul "Bear" Bryant was an advocate of great defenses. He liked to say, "You have to keep from getting beat before you can win." The Bear's teams played great defense, but his teams could also put the ball in the end zone.

I do think offense sells tickets. Most of the big plays in football start with the pass, the favorite being the bomb. But it's hard to win if the team's defense can't stop anybody.

In fact, defenses have become so good we don't see the long run as often as we once did. I still think the long, broken field run is the most exciting play in football. The most boring play in football is the field goal. I didn't say it wasn't important. I didn't say it doesn't win games. I just said there's not a whale of a lot of excitement to it, unless it comes at the end of a game and decides the winner and loser.

If I were a fan of a losing team, I'd vote for offense. I'd rather see my team lose 36-30 than 7-6. But over the long haul, winning sells tickets. It always has, it always will.

CLOSING SHOP 11/11/87

Warner L. Jones Jr. is selling out. In 1935, Warner bought a cattle farm in Oldham County just outside Goshen, and Hermitage Farm began as a thoroughbred operation. After over a half century, Hermitage takes a backseat to no one as a breeding operation. Warner has bred a Kentucky Derby winner and a winner of the Derby Oaks. His horses have won stakes races all over the world, and one of his yearlings is still the highest-priced thoroughbred ever to be sold at public auction. It brought a cool $13.1 million.

This Saturday at Keeneland, Warner Jones will sell his horses at auction. Mares and weanlings with impeccable pedigrees will go under the hammer. Warner Jones is closing his operation. Oh, he'll keep the farm and even a few horses to race, but his gigantic and successful breeding operation will become history.

When Warner Jones started Hermitage Farm, he located well outside the mainstream of the breeding industry in Central Kentucky. Still, he's made it, and made it big. He goes out in glory.

I'm glad Warner is going to race a few horses. He's one of my favorite people, so it'll be nice to see him at the track from time to time. He leaves the breeding business, but he leaves it better than he found it. But then, he's been doing that for thoroughbred racing for over a half century.

OLD RIVALS 12/9/87

Despite the two campuses being located only about 75 miles apart, when Kentucky and Louisville meet in Rupp Arena this Saturday, it will mark only the 19th basketball meeting between these two old neighbors.

They first met back in 1913, then played on a fairly regular basis until after the 1922 season. Then for some reason the series came to a screeching halt. They played only four times in the next 61 years, and each meeting was in some kind of post-season play: the Olympic trials in 1948 and the NCAA tournament in 1951, 1959 and 1983.

The two schools finally got together for a series beginning with the 1983-84 season. It was a home-and-home annual game and the contract was for four years. The series has been so successful that, Saturday, the two schools will begin a new four-year contract.

There's no love lost between the fans of the two schools, but through the first four games, there has been a mutual respect on both sides of the aisle. That's the way it should be. Both have top-of-the-line talent and state-of-the-art coaching. They are just two of the best college basketball teams, year after year, in the country.

A win is a prized possession, but a loss is not the end of the world. There for awhile it was called "the game." Now that the two teams are playing every year, it's just a game. A game, yes, but a big one.

MOVING UP 1/12/88

John Cooper made a lot of friends in Lexington. He came to the University of Kentucky as an assistant on Fran Curci's football staff. John coached the defensive backs, and was good at it. Like most assistant coaches, John wanted to run his own shop. Five years after he came to UK, John got his chance when he was named the head coach at Tulsa. He won. Since nobody expects to make Tulsa the last stop, when Curci was fired at UK, Cooper called his friends to help him get the Kentucky job. Their advice was, "Stay where you are." It might have been good advice. Who knows? Who will ever know?

From Tulsa, he moved to Arizona State and enjoyed more success. Just recently, he moved again, this time to Ohio State. Some of his Lexington friends advised him against the move. "Stay where you are John," they told him, "stay in the land of milk and honey." John didn't listen.

Ironically, his Arizona State team had the same record last season as Ohio State...6-4-1. John got a better job. Ohio State fired Earl Bruce.

I don't blame John Cooper for taking the Buckeye job. To start with, there's the challenge. Then there's the money, reportedly around $340,000 a year. Cooper's timing is right; Arizona State has just put in a new policy that requires all out-of-state students to have a 3.0 grade point average or better, graduate in the upper fourth of their class, and make 23 on the ACT. Given that, John Cooper's choice to go to Ohio State was, I would certainly think, an easy one to make.

NECKTIES 'N SOUR GRAPES 2/2/88

Auburn is a small town. There isn't a whole lot to do in Auburn, so the people at the University have a lot of time to sit around and think.

Auburn's football team is a tough customer to beat, but whether you beat them or not, don't get into a name-calling contest with the University. Syracuse did. Syracuse lost.

Syracuse didn't lose on the football field. It tied Auburn. Actually, it was Auburn that went for a late-game field goal to gain the tie in the Sugar Bowl. Syracuse hinted that Auburn might be lacking in the old fortitude department, going for the tie instead of the win. The two coaches took a few verbal potshots at each other.

But Syracuse couldn't let a sleeping dog lie. A radio station in that city began to collect neckties to send to Auburn coach Pat Dye. They collected about 2,000 of those suckers. Don't you know there were some beauts in there? Auburn fans were irate. The University, however, turned it into something positive. Coach Dye took out his pen, autographed those neckties, sold them for a hundred bucks apiece and donated the money to Auburn's general scholarship fund.

Auburn wasn't through. A Montgomery radio station began collecting grapes, sour grapes, and sent them to Syracuse coach Dick MacPherson. Now those things can get pretty gamey sitting there in the athletics department.

Syracuse came out even in the football game, but has lost every battle with Auburn since.

AND THE TRUTH IS... 3/18/88

I found an article in my files the other day that had been sent to me by a friend who loves to fish. I mean, he's one of those fishing nuts who has always contended that fishermen are much misunderstood.

The article, written by Ben Hall, was published in the Fish and Wildlife Department's magazine *Happy Hunting Ground.*

Mr. Hall must be a real fisherman too. He seems to really have a grasp of the sport. In the article, he sets out to dispel some myths that many of us have about those who are really into fishing. My friend, says Mr. Hall, has flat hit the nail on the head.

No matter what we may think, fishing is not a sport practiced with a pole that has a worm on one end and a fool on the other.

We misunderstand our fishing friends sometimes because we don't understand that for a story to be true, a fishing story does not have to meet the same standards as other stories. In a fishing story, one statement that is strictly factual is all that's required. If a fisherman says, "I went fishing the other day..." the requirement for truth has been met. If that much is true, we should be willing to buy the rest of the story.

Some of us have a mistaken notion that fishermen spend too much time in pursuit of their sport. Those notions are greatly exaggerated. All these stories we hear about fishermen ignoring their wives, leaving the grass uncut and failing to do the chores are much overemphasized. Mr. Hall says they're true, but much overemphasized.

THE NEW NECESSITY 4/4/88

America will crown a college basketball champion tonight in Kansas City. The 64-team field that began the battle for the NCAA title has been reduced to just two. With all these tournament games behind us, I think one thing has become apparent...the three-point shot has brought a tremendous change to the game of college basketball.

We should have spotted that last year when Indiana, with Steve Alford's long-range sharp-shooting, won the national title. But that was the first year of the three-pointer. This year was the second year, and the teams that did the best in post-season play were those teams that had the three-pointer as a part of their regular offense, rather than have a player rush off the bench when a three-pointer was crucial. Coaches spot these things right off and can defense them. The three-point shooter must be a regular.

Coaches are still going to recruit the big people and the quick people. That's still a necessary ingredient to winning, but the player that previously might have been a tad slow, or a tad small, is going to be able to pick and choose his school if he can hit from behind that 19-foot, nine-inch line.

The 45-second shot clock changed the game a little, the three-point shot has changed it a lot. The teams that win from now on will be the teams that do the things they've always done, plus having at least one deadeye from three-point range. It's a must in college basketball these days.

THE LONGEST DAY 4/8/88

College athletes spend a lot of time in their sport. While other students have time to study or lolly-gag around, the athletes spend hours and hours on the practice field.

In college basketball, the hours are getting longer. The first team I heard of that spent extra time on the court was Providence. Dave Gavitt, the Commissioner of the Big East, told me that Providence practiced three times a day. There was an early morning shooting practice, a one-on-one meeting at mid-day, then the regular afternoon practice. Last season, Providence proved to be the sport's Cinderella team, going all the way to the Final Four.

Kentucky's Eddie Sutton, during this past season, found his team shooting a woeful 46 percent from the field. Eddie put in an early morning shooting practice. The Wildcats elevated their field goal accuracy three full percentage points the last part of the season.

Temple was rated the No. 1 team in the nation this season before being waylaid by Duke in the East regional finals. John Chaney holds two practice sessions a day, the first one at an ungodly 5:30 a.m. The players go at it for two-and-a-half hours before being given donuts and coffee. Then they're off to school. Chaney brings them back for regular drills in the afternoon.

If extra practice has worked for at least these three teams, is it the wave of the future in college basketball? I think it is.

CRAZY LOUIE? 7/5/88

There he was, standing outside barn No. 41 in the stable area at Churchill Downs. Louie Roussell was all decked out in his black running suit, holding court with the members of the media, telling everyone about his race horse. Telling everyone that his colt would have a better shot at winning the Kentucky Derby in the hands of Hall of Fame trainer Charlie Whittingham. But the colt wasn't trained by Charlie; he was trained by the man some dubbed "Crazy Louie." Louie's colt didn't win the Derby. He came in third. But Louie's colt won the next two legs of the Triple Crown, the Preakness and the Belmont. Louie kept on saying that he would do the training this year, but sure as shootin', the colt would be under the guidance of Whittingham next year. Well, Charlie won't have the talented race horse next year, either. Crazy Louie sold half-interest in the colt to a Lexington horse farm for seven million smackers, and the colt will hang up his racing shoes at the end of this year. The colt, of course, is Risen Star, the hottest three-year-old in racing.

Louie Roussell and his partner, Ronnie Lamarque, bought the colt as a two-year-old in training for $300,000. There was no long wait getting Risen Star to the races. They got their money back several times over at the races. He's earned over $2 million. You can now add another $7 million. And they still own half the horse. If Louie Roussell is crazy, wouldn't we like to be just as crazy? And just as rich?

UNDERPAID MULTI-MILLIONAIRES 9/27/88

When we see those monstrous six- and even seven-figure salaries the top athletes make these days, it takes our breath, doesn't it?

Well, compared to rock singers and TV stars, athletes come in way down the line. Forbes Magazine picked the top 40 earners in entertainment over the last two years, and only three athletes were ranked on that list. All three are boxers. Heavyweight champ Mike Tyson is the only athlete to make the top 10, ranked eighth, with a two-year income of $50 million. That's pretty far down the line from the top money-maker, Michael Jackson at $97 million, or No. 2 Bill Cosby at $92 million. Sugar Ray Leonard was ranked 21st at $27 million. Sugar Ray is the boxer who comes out of retirement just often enough to keep us from forgetting his name. Sugar Ray is out of retirement right now, but expect an announcement that he's retiring again right after his next fight.

Michael Spinks is the only other athlete on the 40-richest entertainer list, way down there in the No. 38 spot. Tyson knocked his block off when they met. Hey, don't shed any tears for Spinks. He still earned $17 million over the past two years. I still think athletes are overpaid, but if singers and actors are making the kind of bucks they're making, why shouldn't the athlete get those big bucks? In most cases, his career is going to be a lot shorter than the other entertainers.

SNATCHING VICTORY FROM THE JAWS... 2/2/89

Now, I want you to picture this. A basketball team has a two-point lead. It also has possession of the ball. There is only one second left to play. How on earth can that team lose? Well, last week Vanderbilt found a way.

The Vanderbilt fans beat their own basketball team. They began throwing tennis balls onto the court, their way of poking fun at Florida center Dwayne Schintzius, who got into a fight using a tennis racket back before the season began. The tennis balls brought forth a two-shot technical foul against Vandy. The Commodores also had to give up the ball. Ironically, it was Schintzius who hit the free throws to send the game into overtime. Florida won.

It happened to C.M. Newton the day after he accepted the athletics director's job at UK. C.M. was already taking some heat in the Nashville press for announcing his resignation in midseason, so he certainly didn't need a game like that.

If C.M. is catching it down in Music City, he's the toast of the Bluegrass. His hiring has been a boost in Kentucky. You can count me among the many who think it was one of UK's finest hours when they persuaded the former Wildcat to return to his alma mater to head the athletics department. In a year when good news has been in short supply at Kentucky, C.M. Newton was just what the doctor ordered.

C.M.'s nightmare in the Florida game could happen to anybody. They're cracking down on unruly crowds in the SEC. Don't get physical this season, or it could cost your team a game.

SUTTON RESIGNS 3/20/89

Eddie Sutton has had enough. Yesterday he announced that he was resigning as the head basketball coach at Kentucky. I don't think it's any secret that he resigned with a gun to his head. A gun with the hammer cocked. I believe he is relieved that this nightmare is over. He coached for four years at UK, and did so with much success until this past season when the NCAA investigation wrecked the campaign, causing UK to turn in its first losing season in 62 years.

Coach Sutton made his announcement in a live hookup from Lexington to CBS-TV. He said he was leaving for "...the love I have for the University of Kentucky basketball program and the people of the Commonwealth." He also maintained his innocence of the charges that had been brought by the NCAA. Few of us will ever know what a horrendous year this has been for Sutton and his family. There have been vicious stories and rumors, yet, to his credit, Eddie Sutton has handled them without bitterness or anger. Apparently, the burden became too heavy for Eddie, and over the weekend he decided to call it quits.

At 53, Eddie Sutton has a lot of good years of coaching ahead, and he says he wants to continue coaching somewhere. He should. He's very good at it. At Kentucky, he took the Wildcats to the NCAA tournament his first three seasons. His first team won 32 games and came up just one win short of reaching the Final Four. He was voted the national "Coach of the Year."

Eddie Sutton is a nice man and one heck of a basketball coach. If he is innocent of the NCAA charges, he will be vindicated. The program at Kentucky will be hit hard when the punishment is handed down. For those reasons, Sutton's resignation will be a good thing for him, and in the long run, for the UK program.

DUMB JOCK 101 3/29/89

There's just no doubting that everybody seems to enjoy jokes about dumb jocks. Coach George Raveling says he tried to test a recruit by asking him to spell "Mississippi." The recruit asked, "The state or the river?" Pure fiction? Of course, but these things persist. I got one from somewhere the other day that purportedly was an exam given to athletes, asking them to describe certain medical terms. I wonder who sits around with nothing better to do than think up these things.

In this fictitious survey, when asked the medical term "barium," the reply was, "what you do when your pet dies." "Post operative" was described as a "letter carrier," while "minor operation" was a "coal digging company." "Protein" was said to be "in favor of young people." "Nitrate" came to be "lower than the day rate" and "dilate" meant "to live long." "Node" was "to be aware of," and "benign" is "what you are after you are eight."

Somewhere, sometime, the mistaken notion surfaced that athletes were dumb. Dumb jock is almost one word. It takes intelligence just to get into college, yet the jokes persist. They are funny, and I just thought I'd share these with you.

CANDIDATE CAWOOD 5/9/89

John Clay, with tongue firmly in cheek, mentioned it in *The Lexington Herald-Leader*. But I'm serious about this thing. I have a good notion to give C.M. Newton a call and throw my hat into the ring for the Kentucky basketball coaching job. Now, between you and me, I don't expect to get it. What I do expect to get is a raise.

If C.M. Newton will do me a favor and act as if I might be a serious candidate, my raise is virtually guaranteed. It worked for Lute Olson. It worked for P.J. Carlesimo. Why wouldn't it work for me? Lute Olson ought to be on Wall Street. He'd already turned UK down once, but there he was, stuck in the middle of a contract at Arizona. The only way he could get his school to up the ante was to make the boys in the front office think he might ride off to some big basketball school like Kentucky.

When Carlesimo's name came up, C.M. and I may have been the only people in the state who even knew him. Oh, we all knew he had come within a free throw of winning the NCAA championship, but few had actually met P.J.

In one week, *The Herald-Leader* ran three front page stories on the man. The first story informed us that the Seton Hall coach was the first to talk with the UK screening panel. A few days later, the headline read, "Carlesimo Does Things The Right Way." See, we've got his name, and we've seen his picture enough by now to know what he looks like. The last front page story that week read, "Carlesimo Won't Leave Home For UK." Do you think Seton Hall didn't kick in some bucks? Think again. So, consider me a candidate for the job...at least until my raise comes through.

AND THE WAITING CONTINUES 5/15/89

The National Basketball Coaches' Association should at least give the University of Kentucky some kind of plaque. UK is still without a coach, but two members of the Association can thank the University for getting hefty pay raises. Lute Olson and P.J. Carlesimo are a little heavier in the pockets today because UK showed an interest. Terry Holland at Virginia may be about to become the third. He has already said he'd be willing to talk with C.M. Newton after the NCAA hands down its penalties. Virginia is already talking a better deal to Terry.

A new candidate may surface tomorrow. If the Chicago Bulls beat the New York Knicks, the Knicks are out of the pro basketball playoffs. Sources say Knicks' coach Rick Pitino will then be ready to talk to C.M. Right now, Pitino is probably the leading candidate for the job.

I never did think Kentucky would have a hard time hiring a coach. This job has been so special, the top men in the business were clamoring for it. Why the change of heart? Is it the expected penalty? I don't think so. Nowadays, the top coaches make big dollars everywhere, not just at Kentucky and a few other big-name programs. With a big income already, who needs the fishbowl existence one would get at UK? Nobody wants to live under a microscope.

My new candidate for the job is Robert Lindsey. He's the disc jockey who is perched up on a billboard platform. He vows to stay there until Kentucky hires a coach. That's more interest in the job than anybody else has shown.

THE RIGHT MAN 5/17/89

C.M. Newton likes to tell everyone that he feels like he's driving a car without a steering wheel. No doubt, there have been times when C.M. has felt that way. But he knew coming in that he was entering one of the toughest, most challenging battles of his life. The University of Kentucky, C.M.'s alma mater and one of the truly premier basketball programs anywhere, had fallen on hard times. There was no coach, the threat of severe NCAA penalties was hanging overhead, and rumor had it that several of the current players were thinking of leaving. It wasn't an enviable position for anybody, even a man with the kind of strength and character that C.M. possesses. But since taking over officially as UK's athletics director back on April 1, C.M. has proved that he was the right man — perhaps the only man — for the job of rebuilding UK's beleaguered basketball program. C.M. has that soothing effect. And he's believable and trustworthy.

One of the first things he did after the meeting with the NCAA was to go on a whistle-stop speaking tour around the Commonwealth. C.M. wanted to tell Wildcat fans what had happened, where things stood and what to expect. That was a smart idea, because UK needs some positive PR during these trying times. UK will bounce back, and C.M. Newton will be the man to engineer that comeback.

THE DARKEST HOUR 5/22/89

The night is darkest just before the dawn. Hold that thought. Hold it and believe it because this is the darkest hour in Kentucky's proud basketball history. The NCAA handed down some of the most severe penalties on record, penalties that even a program as strong as Kentucky's might need years to overcome. The basketball program is in ashes. To a team already short on talent, the NCAA has ruled that UK's best two players, Chris Mills and Eric Manuel, are ineligible. The two-year ban on post-season tournament play will surely cause other players to transfer, and they will be among the best. Kentucky will not be permitted to give scholarships to fill those vacancies. The team is still without a coach since Eddie Sutton's forced resignation. There's not much to smile about today if you're a Kentucky basketball fan.

Are you still holding the thought? There will be a dawn. Kentucky basketball will be back where it belongs — among the best in the sport. Adolph Rupp, the man who gave us our proud basketball tradition, had a line for hard times like these. He said, "The Maker has assured me that the sun will come up tomorrow." It will.

There are things even the NCAA can't legislate against. We have a good man as the new athletics director...C.M. Newton. He will find us a top coach, a man who cannot only coach winning basketball but who can help unify the legions of fans who are despondent and downcast today. The biggest thing Kentucky has going for it is you. No school has ever had a more loyal or a more supportive group of fans. UK needs you now more than ever before.

During Coach Sutton's troubled ride through the nightmare that was last season, he often rolled out the quote, "Tough times don't last, tough people do." If he left us with nothing else, he left us with some very good advice.

THE SEARCH IS OVER 6/1/89

Robert W. Lindsey, come on down! Get off that billboard, the search is over. The WVLK disc jockey has been leading the watch as Kentucky searched for a new basketball coach. Robert W., you can climb down. Shortly after 10 this morning, Rick Pitino became the head coach at the University of Kentucky. Like most Kentuckians, Robert W. got the news on his radio. However, nobody cheered louder than the man who has made his home on a billboard for more than two weeks now. You're going to like Rick Pitino. To begin with, he brings strong coaching credentials with him. He has been successful in rebuilding programs, and none have been a bigger challenge than he faces with this Kentucky program. He took over a floundering program at Providence College and took it to the Final Four in two years. He comes to UK from the New York Knicks, a team coming off its best season in years. Pitino has a name that should help him in rounding up the kind of recruits it will take to put Kentucky back on top.

Pitino said all the right things at his press conference today. The man could give Norman Vincent Peale a lesson in positive thinking, and after a year of heartbreak, UK fans need to hear something positive. He told us he will put a team on the floor that will get the ball up and down the court. His Kentucky teams will play an up-tempo, fast-paced game. That brought smiles from Kentucky fans who have always appreciated the running game. Pitino says he will put in place a full-court pressing defense, and that will be a new look in Kentucky basketball. Pitino promises action and well-conditioned athletes and that, in time, the Wildcats will once again be competing for the national championship. Well, like I said, Pitino said all the right things. No coach in modern time has come into such a difficult situation at Kentucky. Adolph Rupp had an All-American returning on his first team. Joe B. Hall had three returning starters from an SEC championship team and a dynamite recruiting class coming in. Eddie Sutton inherited virtually the whole team that had made it to the NCAA Final 16 the year before.

Rick Pitino takes over a team that is short in numbers, short in stature and short on talent. He seems to relish the situation. He's been there before. He is the right man at the right time for UK basketball.

In front of a national media contingent, Rick Pitino accepted the University of Kentucky's offer to become the 19th coach in Wildcat basketball history.

GOOD IDEA 6/23/89

An article in last week's issue of *The NCAA News* caught my eye. The headline read, "Notre Dame Athletes Get Advice on How to Handle Media." The article tells of how the top athletes on Notre Dame's defending national championship football team underwent a session with an outside consulting firm in an effort to improve their interviews with the media. Quoting from the article, it reads, "Sixteen players got tips on how to give quotes that get used, how to say what they really mean and even how to be patient when the same dumb question gets asked for the umpteenth time."

This may have been the first time that outside people have been brought in to teach athletes about dealing with the media, but Notre Dame was no pioneer in that area. Joe B. Hall did it years ago. During the Christmas break, when the Kentucky basketball team just about made up the entire student body on campus, Coach Hall got UK professors to counsel the players on media interviews, proper table manners and other social graces.

While the article on Notre Dame is positive, the press roasted Coach Hall. He was trying to turn his players into robots, they said.

Rubbish. It was a good idea when Joe B. Hall came up with the plan several years back and it's a good idea now for Notre Dame. If some of the top CEOs in the country get help on dealing with the media, why shouldn't young college athletes? How things have changed.

NOW RICK, ABOUT THE WAY YOU SPEAK... 6/28/89

Dear Coach:

Everywhere I've traveled around the Commonwealth lately, UK fans are truly excited that you have taken the very difficult job of rebuilding UK's demolished basketball program. It's my understanding that your book, "Born To Coach" that was written while you were in New York, is selling like hotcakes here in Kentucky.

Coach, the only criticism of you that has fallen on my ears is that you talk funny. I guess they mean your New York accent. If you don't mind, let me give you a few pointers before you get a chance to tour our state. Here in Kentucky the towns are pronounced, Versailles...not Ver-sigh, and Athens not Ath-ens. Our state's largest city is pronounced Looa-ville, never Louie-ville...or, heaven forbid, Louis-ville.

Around here, we call that group that did Kentucky in, the NC-Double-A, not the NC-Two-A. The place where the Wildcats play is Rupp Arena, not Arener. When addressing more than one person, it's never you-see, it's y'all, as in y'all come see me. A short distance away can be over yonder, or down the road apiece. Coach, I realize it will take time to master Kentuckyese, but don't worry about talking funny. Just put a few "Ws" on the board and that'll take care of it. People said Adolph Rupp talked funny, but it didn't matter as those wins rolled in. Over in Chapel Hill, they thought Frank McGuire talked funny, but it didn't seem to make much difference after he built the Tar Heels into a power. Good luck to you, coach.

Sincerely,
Cawood Ledford

GREEDY LATE-NIGHT BLUNDER 9/13/89

If a college coach, or athletics director, is against some proposal, you can almost bet the farm that one of the stated reasons is that the players will miss too many classes. I don't think they really care. They prove it everyday.

The Southeastern Conference recently released its television schedule for the coming season. Very proudly, the release out of the conference office hails a new agreement between the SEC and ESPN, the cable network, to televise games every Tuesday.

The games will begin at 9:30 p.m. Eastern Time. Now folks, that's a plain bad idea. To begin with, they'll actually start later than 9:30. Nine-thirty is when the telecast will start. The games will start several minutes later.

Now, if Florida plays Ole Miss, and that happens to be the first Tuesday televised game on the schedule, those Florida players are going to get back to Gainesville in the wee hours of the morning. Do you think those players are going to make an 8 a.m. class? No, and they shouldn't be expected to. The Big Ten has had one of those 9:30 week-night deals for several seasons, and each season Indiana's Bobby Knight rails against it. He rails against it for all the right reasons, because it's simply not fair to the players.

Of course, fair has nothing to do with it. When it comes to players missing classes or money, in college sports, money wins every time.

COUNTING DOWN 9/26/89

Eighteen days and counting. The college basketball coaches will get the green light in 18 days, on Oct. 15, to begin practice. Most of them have the players huffing and puffing through running and weightlifting now, but they can't really get down to the nitty gritty of X's and O's until the 15th. For several weeks now, my mail has been heavy with those pre-season basketball brochures. Soon, the big, thick ones will start coming in. The first ones are teasers, a few pages of optimistic prose about the up-coming season.

Let me read you the first two paragraphs from the UK pre-season prospectus. "A funny thing happened to the University of Kentucky basketball team last season. It lost. It lost more games than it won for the first time since 1927. It lost two players after graduation, and three more after probation. It lost an entire coaching staff. It lost any chance of being on TV next season, and it lost precious scholarships and post-season play for the next two seasons.

"After losing so much, then why are Kentucky basketball fans feeling like winners these days? Two words. Rick Pitino."

Now, those words were written by UK people, paid to look on the brighter side. But I find them extremely accurate.

Not in my lifetime has a Kentucky coach faced such a challenge. The story by UK says three players left. If you count Eric Manuel, it's four. There aren't many scholarship players around this season. When they took the team picture a couple of weeks ago, there were more people in civies than in UK basketball uniforms. It's going to be a long winter, but a very interesting one at Kentucky.

BIG RED 10/5/89

Gus Koch called from Claiborne Farm with bad news: the great Secretariat was dead. The news came Tuesday. He was 19.

It might sound trivial to eulogize a horse, but Secretariat wasn't just any horse. He was certainly the best of his time, maybe the best that ever was.

I'd be hard put to name my favorite football or basketball or baseball player, but in race horses, it's easy. It's Secretariat by a mile.

To start with, he was, and is to this day, the best-looking horse I ever laid eyes on. But beauty is as beauty does. Secretariat did. He could literally run a hole in the wind. He broke last in the 1973 Kentucky Derby, then circled the whole field to win. To this day, that was the fastest Derby in history. He went on to win the Preakness. He still had to go on to win the Belmont to become the first Triple Crown winner in a quarter of a century. In those 25 years, seven good horses had won the Derby and the Preakness. It was the long mile and a half at Belmont that got them all.

Secretariat not only won it, he ran one of the most incredible races in history. Through the stretch, he began to draw away from the field. He led by 10 lengths, then 20, and at the wire he was 31 lengths in front. It was the fastest Belmont of all time.

I don't expect to see another Secretariat in my time. Claiborne president Seth Hancock gave me two of Secretariat's shoes this past summer. I'll always treasure those shoes. They came from the fastest feet that ever stepped onto a race track. The big red horse is gone. But Secretariat, thanks for the memories.

T.K.O. BY MOM 10/16/89

Even though I don't have any influence on the voting for "Mother of the Year," I'd like to nominate somebody. I'd like to nominate Minna Wilson of Great Britain. Minna is 62, and she showed the great courage recently that only a mother, defending her young, can show. When Minna saw her little boy being battered and beaten by an assailant, she rushed to the rescue. Minna took off one of her high-heeled pumps and went after the attacker. With that spiked heel, she smashed the brute in the head, opening up a wound that sent the assailant to the hospital.

The only thing was, Minna's little boy happened to be in the boxing ring at the time, fighting for a shot at the British light heavyweight title.

Tony Wilson was on the ropes. Steve McCarthy had knocked him down for the eight count once, and it looked like it was over for Tony. That's where mom came in. Minna came rushing from the audience, jumped into the ring, took off her shoe and went after McCarthy. When she got through with him, McCarthy was unable to continue and Minna's boy Tony was declared the winner. Sadly, Minna Wilson has been barred from any future bouts Tony may have. Barred by that very son she was trying to protect. Tony says mom will just have to stay at home for any of his bouts from now on. But what about shoeless Minna for "Mother of the Year?" She at least ought to get a shoe contract out of this thing.

SHADY DEALINGS 11/14/89

Kentucky lost out and Louisville was caught with egg on its face. UK's new coach, Rick Pitino, thought he had a genuine chance to go into Denny Crum's backyard and pick off Dwayne Morton, the state's best basketball player.

Wednesday, Morton signed on with U of L. A Louisville TV station indicated that Denny Crum had met with Morton and his mother on Monday night, a direct NCAA violation. Crum denied the meeting. He hadn't met with Morton, but he had met with Morton's mother. That's still a violation. Crum insists that he didn't know that it was. Louisville isn't likely to get any punishment from the NCAA, at least nothing more severe than a reprimand, and that's the same as nothing. Louisville got Morton, but Louisville got embarrassed.

The villain of the whole piece has turned out to be Morton's coach at Central High School, Ralph Johnson. Most of Pitino's wrath has been directed at him. Pitino believes that Johnson told Crum of Morton's decision while telling him he didn't know what Morton would do.

The delay, the waiting game, cost Pitino a top recruit in Mississippi. Stephen Davis got tired of waiting at the church for word from Pitino and signed with Ole Miss.

Pitino will be more wise to the ways of Kentucky politics, even basketball politics, next time.

Crum should have known he was breaking the rules, but I honestly don't think he did. The real mystery in this whole charade is the role Ralph Johnson played. He's changed his story so often that we aren't likely to ever really know what happened.

HELLO PITINO-BALL 11/28/89

A feisty coach and a bunch of feisty no-name players open the Kentucky basketball season tonight against Ohio University in Rupp Arena. UK Athletics Director C.M. Newton, who came here as a freshman in 1948, says this is the worst talent Kentucky has put on the court in all those years. The NCAA penalties have gored the UK program. For his first game as the Kentucky coach, Rick Pitino has only eight scholarship players. He has only one starter returning after three others exercised their option to transfer. No player is taller than 6-8. Short seems to be the best word to describe the first year of Pitino-ball. The Cats are short on experience, short in numbers, short in size and short on talent. With so many negatives, why is everybody so enthusiastic about the new season?

Let me count the ways. This will be one of the best-conditioned teams in UK history. Coach Pitino was appalled at the poor condition of the players when they reported for practice, so it has been run, run, run since then. Recently, the UK coach pronounced the team ready for battle. It will have to be physically superior to play Pitino-ball. The new coach says his team will play a full-court swarming defense and will change those defenses to suit certain situations. It will resemble a Chinese fire drill at times, but it should be exciting. On offense, Pitino wants his team to run and to shoot the three-pointer whenever the shot is there. This should play right into the hands of Richie Farmer and Derrick Miller, and maybe even junior Reggie Hanson. Reggie has never taken a trey, but he's been putting them up in practice. And he vows he'll fire away when he gets the opportunity from three-point range.

This is a new beginning for Kentucky basketball. Tonight, the Cats start over, start to rebuild the program. It is hard to see many wins this season in the face of an extremely difficult schedule. But it's a beginning, a beginning that will eventually carry the Cats back to the top.

AN ERA ENDS 12/4/89

The Jerry Claiborne Era is over. He has resigned as the football coach at the University of Kentucky and, at age 61, announced he was leaving the coaching profession. During his eight seasons at UK, the Wildcats won 41 games, lost 46 and tied three. To look at Claiborne's won-lost record is deceiving. He didn't win a game his first season in 1982. That club went 0-10-1. But the very next year, Claiborne guided the Wildcats to a 6-5-1 record that included a trip to the Hall of Fame Bowl. The next year the Wildcats prospered with a 9-3 record that included a win over Wisconsin in their second consecutive journey to the Hall of Fame. His last five Kentucky teams flirted with a .500 worksheet.

However, Jerry Claiborne's eight years cannot even be measured by wins and losses. That would be unfair. When he came to his alma mater in 1982, the program was virtually out of control. Players were making more headlines off the field than on it. Claiborne brought an old-fashioned discipline with him, and the players soon learned that the rules were for one and all. If a sub or a star broke them, he was sent packing. Claiborne brought stability to the program, not just with discipline, but by putting the word "student" back into the term "student-athlete." He produced only seven All-SEC players during his eight-year tenure, but he led the league over that time frame in academic all-conference players. In 1989, Kentucky led the country in graduating its football players.

Jerry didn't always recruit the best players, and it was the dreaded recruiting duties that finally drove him out of coaching. But he brought in good quality young men who wanted to earn a college education, and he made them competitive on the football field. Taking notice of the shabby practice facilities at UK, Jerry engineered the drive to raise more than $5.5 million to build the E.J. Nutter Center, one of the finest training facilities in the country.

LUCKY NEWTON STRIKES AGAIN

1/8/90

His given name is Charles Martin but how he's been around for 60 years without being called "Lucky" is beyond me. C.M. Newton has to be the luckiest man alive.

The former Wildcat basketball player who came home just nine months ago to take over as the director of athletics produced another stroke of genius today when he signed Bill Curry to coach the UK football team. This is the second high-profile coach Newton has produced in his short career back at his alma mater.

Bill Curry comes to Kentucky from that Southern football factory called Alabama. The new UK coach brings glowing credentials to the job. He has been a head coach for 10 years, seven at Georgia Tech and the last three at Alabama. This past season, Curry guided Alabama to the SEC crown and was named the league's coach of the year.

Curry enjoyed much success at Alabama with a three-year record of 26-10. He took the Crimson Tide to three-straight bowls. But it wasn't all smooth sailing for the Curry family in Tuscaloosa. He was resented by some for not being an Alabama man, for not beating Auburn and for not winning them all. That discontent at Alabama made it possible for UK to hire him.

Most coaches say all the right things at the press conferences right after they're hired, and Curry was no exception. He talked of championship teams and championship programs. He talked of class. He praised his predecessor, Jerry Claiborne. Curry comes across as intense, yet open.

C.M. Newton thinks he has hired the best two coaches in the country. I agree. But when you consider that C.M. was turned down by two other basketball coaches before he hired Pitino and was spurned by at least one football coach before he got Curry's name on the dotted line, he has to be the luckiest man alive. If I see Newton in Vegas, I'll follow him right to the gaming tables and stack my chips right up beside his.

SLICK RICK STRIKES AGAIN 6/25/90

P.T. Barnum would have been proud of Rick Pitino. The old master showman must have been smiling down from that big circus in the sky last season as the new UK coach brought showbiz to basketball in the Bluegrass. Pitino made going to a UK game equal to a trip to Disneyland.

Rick waited for the lazy days of summer to play his trump card. Earlier this month he hired Bernadette Locke, making her the first woman coach on the staff of a Division I men's basketball team. The phones have been ringing off the hooks ever since. Chris Cameron, Director of UK Sports Information, says up to 30 calls a day are coming into his office requesting interviews with Bernadette.

Pitino insists this is no publicity stunt, that Locke was hired because she was the best qualified candidate to replace Ralph Willard after Ralph left to take over as head coach at Western Kentucky. Bernadette is young and attractive, but she also brings solid credentials to her new job. She was an All-American at Georgia, and has spent six years on the coaching staff of the Lady Bulldogs.

Locke has already appeared on "CBS This Morning" and is scheduled for other national TV appearances. Since signing with UK, she is the most visible assistant coach in the country.

That makes her unique. By the very nature of the game, assistant coaches are seldom seen. The head coach takes all the bows. By being the first woman to coach in a men's program, Locke is a pioneer. She is well-spoken and poised. She may be the only coach in college basketball who dresses sharper than Pitino. Not only is she gaining national exposure now, but even after the season starts she will be the focus of attention, being the only woman on the bench. If Pitino had in mind taking some of the spotlight away from himself, he's done it. Bernadette Locke has brought a breath of fresh air to the Kentucky program. She will be welcomed with open arms.

WEEP NO MORE 6/17/91

The most famous Kentuckian died Saturday. Albert Benjamin Chandler was 92. He was known the world over as "Happy" and if ever a name fit, that one fit the man. But to me, he was always Governor.

I met him 38 years ago at a Kentucky basketball game, and the last time I saw him was in Rupp Arena this last season. Others, far more eloquent than I, can speak to his contributions as a leader and a statesman. Sports played a tremendous role in Governor Chandler's long life. He was commissioner of baseball, the highest office in sports in his time. It was during his watch that baseball broke the color line. He was a great friend and confidant to Adolph Rupp, and all the coaches that followed at UK. At the end of Eddie Sutton's first season after Eddie had won 32 games, Governor Chandler wrote him a letter that contained only one word..."unpack."

Governor Chandler was an all-sports star at Transylvania, and while he was attending Harvard Law School he scouted that school's football team for Centre College. In 1921, Centre pulled off one of the biggest upsets in college football history by beating Harvard 6-0. Governor Chandler wanted most to be a coach. While coaching the Centre freshman team, the head coach resigned. Happy figured if he beat Transylvania with his team to go undefeated, he'd get the job. Centre led 13-7 with time just for one more play when the Transylvania quarterback threw one a mile for a touchdown. With no time left, the extra point gave Transy a 14-13 win. Happy didn't get the job. The rest, as they say, is history. But that Transy quarterback always sent the same message to Happy at Christmas. It read: "Remember me. I'm the man who made you governor." That message is one all Kentuckians are thankful for.

Governor Chandler loved Kentucky, and Kentuckians. The feeling was mutual. Good bye, old friend. We'll miss you. And we love you.

FREDDIE'S FINALLY FLIPPED 6/25/91

Prognosticators are a dime a dozen. Whether it's at the racetrack or the stadium, there are plenty of people picking the winners and losers. The hottest gypsy with the crystal ball is UK quarterback Freddie Maggard. It seems Freddie has been picking the final record of UK's basketball team for the past two years and has been doing it with amazing accuracy. Two years ago, when everyone thought the Cats would be lucky to finish with 10 wins, Freddie looked over the schedule, filled in the wins and losses, signed the schedule and gave it to his good friend on the basketball team, John Pelphrey. Freddie predicted the Wildcats would finish 15-13. Their final record was 14-14. That established Maggard as a soothsayer, but anyone can get lucky from time to time. When Freddie made his selections again last year and predicted that the basketball Cats would finish with a 23-5 record, everybody laughed. Laughed until the Cats posted a 22-6 worksheet. Freddie has been so accurate over two years running that we're all beginning to count on him to gaze into the future and tell us how the basketball team will fare. The "Pride of Cumberland" has come out with his predictions for the 1991-92 season. The numbers read 29 wins and two losses. Now wait a minute. I know Freddie suffered a shoulder injury last fall, but I didn't know he had suffered brain damage. According to "Freddie the Greek," the Cats will lose on the road to Tennessee and LSU. That's it.

If what Freddie says is true and the Cats do finish with 29 wins, not only will he be revered forever as an absolute wizard in the basketball predicting business, but Kentucky will find itself No. 1 in the nation.

Freddie Maggard has been so close in his prognostications for the roundball Wildcats over the past two seasons that we have no choice but to give him the benefit of the doubt. But, I still can't help but believe that Freddie has finally flipped.

WONDERFUL NEWS 8/21/91

Louisville's football program has passed UK's. We have Bill Curry's word on that. The Kentucky coach said last week that, "...Louisville is ahead of UK." That's wonderful news to Kentucky fans. I'm not being facetious...it is, and here's why.

If Louisville can produce a winning football program, anybody can. I don't want to hear anymore of this garbage that it is impossible to have a winning program in Kentucky. When Howard Schnellenberger took over at U of L for the 1985 season, the program was in the pits. The Cardinals were one of the worst teams in all of Division I-A. Last year, Schnellenberger's sixth at U of L, his team raced to a 10-1-1 season, earned the school's first major bowl bid and pounded proud Alabama 34-7 in the Fiesta Bowl. Howard has built the top program in the state despite having the worst stadium in Division I-A. He has upgraded the pitiful practice facilities he found, but they are still located off campus. He has been able to recruit only a handful of the top prep stars from the state of Kentucky. Louisville's football success should put to rest forever the myth that it is impossible to build a top program in this state.

And here's another reason to applaud Louisville's football success. Kentucky fans have been the most patient in all of college football. They have given great support to a mediocre program for years. I saw a headline in an old *Lexington Herald-Leader* while leafing through a scrapbook the other day. It read, "The World's Greatest Fans Support UK Football Through...Thin and Thin." How true. Kentucky fans may tolerate mediocrity in the SEC, but they won't stand for being second fiddle in the state. I applaud Bill Curry for telling it like it is. U of L has passed Kentucky.

Now it's time for all of us to do something about it.

CAWOOD'S
AWARDS

CAWOOD'S SPORTS AWARDS

In 1979, when Cawood moved to Lexington to start his own business, he began a weekly feature with his radio comments known as his Sports Awards. The awards were based on humorous or odd stories dealing with the world of sports. He began each segment with, "I've researched the fine print and rifled the waste basket for this week's sports awards." In keeping with that tradition, "It's time for the Sports Awards!"

THE BEST OF '79

The Can't-Seem-To-Run Award to Shapely Miss, a thoroughbred race horse. The horse's owner, Frank Guzowski, is suing the Detroit Race Course for $100,000. It seems that when the starting gate opened all the horses bolted for the lead — except Shapely Miss. According to Guzowski, his horse never had a chance. Somebody had tied her tail to the starting gate.

The Heavenly Quote Award to Lou Holtz of Arkansas. Everyone knows how much pressure coaches are under to win and run a clean program. According to Lou, "Some say God never sends you more than you can handle. But God may be overestimating my ability."

The Are-You-Kidding Award to Frank Layden, NBA executive. While Frank was coaching the Atlanta Hawks, he gave each player a basic information sheet to fill out. Beside one question that asked "church preference?" Layden swears a player penciled in "red brick."

The Best-Quote Award to Yogi Berra. Yogi stopped at a pizza parlor one night on his way home to order a small pizza. The waitress asked Yogi if he wanted his pizza cut into four pieces or eight.

"Four," Yogi replied. "I don't think I can eat eight."

THE BEST OF '81

The Best-Quote Award to Kentuckian Lee Rose, basketball coach at South Florida. Lee's team took a beating, losing to the nation's top-ranked team, North Carolina, 75-39. Lee said he didn't call any timeouts during the late stages of the contest. Why? Because he didn't want the crowd to know who the coach was.

The Best-Comeback Award to Dr. J., Julius Erving. After learning that Boston Celtics' general manager Red Auerbach was quoted as saying that Dr. J. kept one eye on his man and one eye on the basket, the good Doctor said he kept both eyes on his man. He said the basket hasn't moved yet.

The If-You've-Got-It-Flaunt-It Award to Willie Nelson, the country music star. Willie recently bought his own golf course. When asked what the par was on his course, Willie said it was whatever he wanted it to be.

"This hole right here is a par 47," Willie quipped. "Yesterday, I birdied that sucker."

The Best-Quote Award to Joe DiMaggio, former New York Yankee. The Hall of Famer was asked what his salary would be during this day and age of free agency and big spending. Joe said if he were to sit down with Yankees' owner George Steinbrenner, he would say, "George, you and I are about to become partners."

The Way-With-Words Award to golfer Chi Chi Rodriguez. Chi Chi says for most amateur golfers, "The best wood in the bag is the pencil."

THE BEST OF '82

The Best-Quote Award to Dodgers' manager Tom Lasorda. When asked what terms pitching whiz Fernando Valenzuela of Mexico might settle for in his upcoming contract negotiations, Lasorda said, "He wants Texas back."

The Best-Quote Award to Abe Lemons, the comedian who coaches the University of Texas basketball team. In Cincinnati recently for a game against Xavier, reporters asked Abe what he intended to do while he was in town. Abe said, "Zone Xavier...and get something to eat."

The Best-Quote Award to Lee Trevino. After Super Mex was hit by lightning on the golf course a few years ago, he devised a plan for protection in the future. Next time he's caught in a storm on the links, Trevino says he'll take out his 1-iron and stick it straight up in the air. Lee says, "Even God can't hit a 1-iron."

The Best-Quote Award to Abe Lemons, former basketball coach at Texas. He was fired from his job by athletics director DeLoss Dodds. Abe said he didn't have any hard feelings though. But he's going to buy a glass-bottomed car so he can watch the look on Dodds' face when he runs over him.

THE BEST OF '83

The Friendly Skies Award to Vanderbilt Coach C.M. Newton. Asked why he always sits in the very last seat on Vandy's 44-seat chartered plane, C.M. answered, "I've never heard of a plane that's backed into a mountain."

The Best-Quote Award to Bill Frieder, basketball coach at the University of Michigan. Asked about his chances of winning back-to-back road games at Illinois and Purdue,

Frieder said he had a better chance of finding Jimmy Hoffa.

The Putting-It-In-Perspective Award to Ohio University basketball coach Danny Nee. Before his team played Kentucky, Nee said he knew what a tough job coach Joe B. Hall had. Coach Nee said, "I know the pressure that's on him. But I tell you, if God went down there, He'd have trouble too."

The Last-Laugh Award to Jim Valvano, coach of the national champions, North Carolina State. In a showdown with a referee, the official warned Valvano, "If you say anything, I'll give you a technical."

Valvano asked, "What if I think something?"

"That's OK," said the referee.

"I think you stink," answered Valvano.

The One-Man's-Opinion Award to Doug Rader, manager of the Texas Rangers. Doug doesn't share every coach's enthusiasm for players lifting weights. He says, "Lifting weights is great...if you want to pick up a jeep."

The Lighter-Side Award to stock car driver Neil Bonnett. Neil has a 300-horsepower motor on his light fishing boat. He says, "When you hook a bass at 100 miles an hour, it takes the fight right out of him."

The Best-Quote Award to boxer Tex Cobb. Old Tex took such a beating from Larry Holmes last November, Howard Cosell decided to stop announcing boxing. Tex says he'd go 15 more rounds with Holmes if it would get Cosell off the football broadcasts.

The Best-Quote Award to Jim Valvano, coach at North Carolina State. On a recent radio program with me, Valvano said after he moved from Iona to North Carolina State and lost twice to rival North Carolina, he got a note from a fan that read, "If you lose again to North Carolina, I'll kill your dog."

Valvano wrote back, "I don't have a dog."

A few days later, UPS delivered a dog to Valvano's house with a note attached. It said, "Here's your dog...but don't get too attached to him."

The-Sharper-Than-A-Serpent's-Tooth Award to Mike Fuller, players' representative for the Cincinnati Bengals. On learning that Gene Upshaw had been named Executive Director of the Players' Association, Fuller said, "It's like putting a sixth-grade kid in charge of the space program."

The We-Ain't-Had-Our-Bat-Yet Award to a seven-year-old small fry baseball team in Georgia. In the state tournament, East Cherokee defeated Rossville 77-23. Actually, East Cherokee had to pull it out in the last inning. It did, with 58 runs.

The Best-Quote Award to Billy Gardner, manager of the lowly Minnesota Twins. Billy says things are going so bad for him this year that if he bought a pumpkin farm, they'd cancel Halloween.

The Tell-It-Like-It-Is Award to Pittsburgh Steeler quarterback Cliff Stoudt. After throwing three interceptions in a game, Stoudt was asked if he had learned anything. He said he learned how to tackle.

THE BEST OF '84

The Tell-It-Like-It-Is Award to Marino Casem, football coach at Alcorn State. He says in the East, college football is a cultural experience. On the West coast, it's a tourist attraction. In the Midwest, it's cannibalism.

And in the South, it's a religion. Casem says in Dixie, "Saturday is a holy day."

The Best-Story Award to Oklahoma City coach Abe Lemons. He swears he knows a coach who hired two assistants — a psychiatrist and a hair dresser. He says the hair dresser is still there. The psychiatrist went crazy.

The Tongue-In-Cheek Award to Indiana basketball coach Bobby Knight. Asked what part of coaching he enjoyed most?

"Dealing with the writers," Knight replied. "After the demands of the game, my mind needs a rest."

The Chip-Off-The-Old-Block Award to Nebraska's basketball coach Moe Iba. Moe used a zone defense to beat Missouri on the road.

But those who know Moe's daddy, the legendary basketball coach Hank Iba, know he never used a zone while coaching. Moe said he got his dad's approval to use the zone...and he's still in the will.

The Tell-It-Like-It-Is Award to Sonny Smith, basketball coach at Auburn. The school's alumni picked up the mortgage payments on football coach Pat Dye's expensive home. But the offer didn't extend to Sonny's place of residence. Sonny says Auburn offered him a double-wide mobile home, but told him not to take the wheels off.

The Tell-It-Like-It-Is Award to Herb Brooks, the coach of the New York Rangers. Herb says on his first trip to New York, a thief stole his wife's purse and all her credit cards.

But Herb never reported it. He claims the thief spends less than his wife does.

The Dale Carnegie Award to Ron Davis, a pitcher for the Minnesota Twins. Ron's mad at the press. He says it made too much of his criticism of the club for trading away top players.

"All I said was that the trades were stupid and dumb," Ron said. "They took that and blew it all out of proportion."

The Sharper-Than-A-Serpent's-Tooth Award to San Francisco baseball fans. They like asking, "What do Michael Jackson and the Giants have in common?"

Knowing that the Giants make so many errors, the answer becomes obvious. They both wear gloves on one hand — for no apparent reason.

The Sharper-Than-A-Serpent's-Tooth Award to Lou Holtz. Lou left Arkansas to coach at Minnesota this season. About Fayetteville, Ark., Holtz says, "It's not the end of the world, but you can see it from there."

The Best-Sense-Of-Humor Award to the late Walter Alston. There were quite a few eulogies about this fine man and former manager of the L.A. Dodgers when he died recently. The Sober Skipper had a lighter side too, like the baseball he gave his grandson the day he was born.

He wrote on the ball, "May you have the strength of Ruth, the speed of Mantle, the finesse of Reese...and the good looks of your grandfather."

The Things-Can-Always-Get-Worse Award to Earlham coach Ed Clemmer. Things have gone badly at Earlham. Clemmer said he called the suicide hotline and they told him it was the only right call he'd made all day.

Still depressed, he walked into a local lounge. The management promptly threw him out. They told him they were trying to have a happy hour!

The Tell-It-Like-It-Is Award to Jim Greenidge, public relations man for the New England Patriots. Greenidge, who weighs over 320 pounds, said he knew he was overweight when he went to a fried chicken restaurant and ordered meals for the entire team.

"Is that to go," the attendant asked, "or do you want to eat it here?"

THE BEST OF '86

The Zinger Award to Sonny Smith, basketball coach at Auburn.

Sonny never misses a chance to stick it to his friend and colleague Wimp Sanderson, coach at cross-state rival Alabama. Sonny says it takes 15 muscles to smile and 65 muscles to frown. He says that leads him to believe that Wimp is suffering from muscle fatigue.

THE BEST OF '87

The Poison-Pen Award to Larry Guest, columnist for *The Orlando Sentinel.* Referring to Auburn running back Brent Fullwood and the fact that he was eligible to play in the Citrus Bowl even though he hadn't attended class since early fall, Guest wrote, "Auburn's giving Fullwood's professors tickets to the Citrus Bowl so they can finally see him in person."

The Good-Old-Yankee-Know-How Award to Paul Roach, athletics director at Wyoming. After the Cowboys' football coach resigned, Roach appointed himself as the one-man search committee. After looking high and low for the best candidate, Roach found him. He hired himself.

The One-Man's-Opinion Award to Billy Tubbs, basketball coach at Oklahoma. Asked what effect the new three-point goal might have on recruiting, Tubbs said it might drive up the price on guards.

The Best-Comeback Award to Frank Broyles, athletics director at Arkansas. Asked whether he'd like his football coach, Ken Hatfield, just as much if the Razorbacks won only half their games, Broyles replied, "Sure I would, and I'd miss him too."

The Truth-Hurts Award to Gene Mauch, manager of the California Angels. While Don Drysdale was throwing his high hard ones in the majors, he was also accused of throwing the spit ball. When Mauch was asked about Drysdale as a broadcaster, Mauch said, "Very good for a man who's had two fingers in his mouth all his life."

The Clothes-Do-Make-The-Man Award to Tom Kelly, manager of the Minnesota Twins. This season he'll be wearing No. 10 on his uniform instead of his usual No. 41. Kelly said when he thought about it, he realized all the women would be saying, "There goes Tom Kelly. He's a 10."

The One-Man's-Meat Award to Ed Murphy, the successful first year coach at Ole Miss. Ed says that with the competitiveness of the Southeastern Conference, soon every team in the league will finish the conference race with a 9-9 record. Ed says he'll get a raise, but Eddie Sutton will get fired.

The Best-Quote Award to Benny Dees, basketball coach at New Orleans. His team didn't go far in the NCAA but Benny left everybody smiling. In fact, the former Alabama assistant predicted his team wouldn't go very far. He said his daddy told him there were two things that never lasted long: a dog that chased cars and a team that couldn't shoot free throws.

The In-Fashion Award to broadcaster Bob Costas. Commenting on the multicolored sports coat worn by Alabama coach Wimp Sanderson, Costas said he was glad to see that Pinky Lee's estate had finally been settled.

The Golden-Typewriter Award to Alan Greenburg, a columnist for a Connecticut paper. Covering the Celtics-Lakers playoff, Alan wrote that actress Dyan Cannon stood out on the sidelines wearing a zebra-striped skirt. Alan said it obviously came from a small zebra.

The Just-What-The-Doctor-Ordered Award to radio announcer Johnny Most, play-by-play man for the Boston Celtics. Johnny went to the team physician and complained of a hearing loss. He had been suffering with the problem about a year and a half. The good doctor cleared it right up. He removed a radio earplug from Johnny's ear.

The Looking-Into-The-Future Award to Abe Lemons, basketball coach at Oklahoma City. Abe's not looking ahead to retirement. He says the trouble with retirement is you never get a day off!

The To-Tell-The-Truth Award to Alvin Dark, a former major league player and manager. Dark was always known as a deeply religious man. He says the Lord taught him to love everybody. But he admits the last people he learned to love were the sportswriters.

The Yogi Berra Award to Fernando Valenzuela, pitcher for the Los Angeles Dodgers. Fernando is from Mexico and is still trying to get a grip on the English language. Asked recently how important the second half of the season was to the struggling Dodgers, Fernando answered, "Very important. There is no third half."

The Everything-Is-Relative Award to Harry Caray, long-time baseball announcer who calls the action for the Chicago Cubs. Thrice married, Caray says he never realized how short a month was until he started paying alimony.

The Way-With-Words Award to Terry Malley, coach at Santa Clara. He says there are two things his defensive linemen won't do: windows or rush the passer.

The Best-Comparison Award to Abe Lemons, basketball coach at Oklahoma City. Abe believes coaching is tougher than practicing medicine.

"Doctors bury their mistakes," Abe said. "We have ours on scholarship."

The Mother's-Love Award to Kathy Bosworth. She's the mom of Brian Bosworth, the not-so-loved linebacker with the Seattle Seahawks. Kathy says the Boz was her third child. If he had been her first, he would have been an only child.

THE BEST OF '88

The Life-After-Baseball Award to Ron Luciano, a former umpire in the American League. Luciano says being an umpire is a lot like being king — it prepares you for nothing.

The Wheel-Of-Fortune Award to Tony Wallingford, basketball coach at Mulligan College. In the dressing room before a game, Tony was into his pep talk. He told his players what it takes to win.

"The first letter is D," Tony said. When nobody said anything, Tony continued, "The second letter is E." By the time he got to F one of his players wanted to know if he could buy a vowel.

The Golden-Typewriter Award to Glenn Dickey, columnist for *The San Francisco Chronicle.* Commenting on the uproar over the firing of Jimmy the Greek for his racial remarks, Dickey suggests we should remember the good things about the Greek.

He wrote, "He made Phyllis George cry and he punched Brent Musberger."

The Honesty-Is-The-Best-Policy Award to Bob Woolf, Larry Bird's agent. Woolf is in negotiations with the Boston Celtics trying to work out Bird's new contract.

Woolf says, "Larry's not greedy, but I am."

The Lighter-Side Award to Florida State coach Bobby Bowden. Speaking of the perils of recruiting, Bobby said his private plane got caught in a bad thunderstorm. When he asked the pilot how it was going, the pilot said there was good news and there was bad news. The bad news is, we're lost. The good news is, we're making good time.

The Lighter-Side Award to Abe Lemons, coach at Oklahoma City. Abe says a couple of disgruntled alumni dropped by his office and wanted to buy out his contract. He says the deal fell through when neither had change for a $20!

The High-Expectations Award to Speedy Morris, basketball coach at LaSalle. He said when the phone rang at his house one morning and his wife told him it was *Sports Illustrated*, he cut himself shaving and fell down the stairs trying to get to the phone. When he picked it up, a voice on the phone was saying, "...for just 75 cents an issue..."

The Truth-Pure-And-Simple Award to Joe Dean, athletics director at LSU. Old String Music could have been describing just about anyone's fans when he said, "People want LSU to be like Harvard during the week and play like Oklahoma on Saturday."

The Best-Thank-You-Note Award to Brian Fisher, pitcher for the Pittsburgh Pirates. After undergoing surgery on his shoulder, he sent the surgeon a dozen golf balls with a note saying, "One good slice deserves another."

The Putting-Things-In-Perspective Award to Abe Lemons, basketball coach. After a losing game in which his best player scored just one point, Abe supposedly said to his star, "I want to put this in perspective so that you'll understand it. Tonight you scored one more point than a dead man."

The-Secret-For-Success Award to Jim Crews, basketball coach at Evansville. Crews says all you have to do to last a long time in coaching is look like Robert Redford, be as funny as Johnny Carson, have skin as thick as an elephant's and win as often as the Globetrotters.

The Ask-A-Dumb-Question Award to somebody at a recent panel of trainers in Lexington. The question was, "What distinguishes a really good horse from the others?"

Jimmy Jones, former trainer for Calumet Farm said, in his opinion, the really good ones could run faster.

The Good-Idea-Gone-Bad Award to Tommy Lasorda, manager of the Los Angeles Dodgers. Tommy says he took second baseman Steve Sax to the race track and the two of them didn't cash a ticket for five-straight races. But after every race, the people in front of them were dividing money, a whole bunch of money. Lasorda said he gave Sax a $10 bill and told him to stick with that group. When they got in line, he was to get in line and take the same thing they did. In 15 minutes, Sax came back with three roast beef sandwiches.

The Golden-Rule Award to 40-year-old boxer George Foreman. George said he didn't do well in school because he just couldn't get up in time to attend class. He says if school had started at four in the afternoon, he'd have been a college graduate today.

The Looking-On-The-Brighter-Side Award to Bill Fitch, coach of the New Jersey Nets in the NBA. Fitch says he's independently wealthy. He says he has enough money to last him the rest of his life. Provided he dies tomorrow.

The Last-Word Award to Magic Johnson of the Los Angeles Lakers. Magic and Coach Pat Riley were talking about Kareem Abdul Jabbar's absence this season after so many years. Riley said to Magic, "We'll find out now what kind of player you are."

Magic replied, "Yeah, and we'll find out what kind of coach you are."

THE BEST OF '90

The Good-To-Be-Among-Friends Award to golfer Lee Trevino. Super Mex recently joined the Seniors' Tour and is performing well. He said he prefers the older tour to the regular tour. On the regular tour, all the players are drinking potassium-rich orange juice and eating bananas. On the Seniors' Tour, he says he can still go into the locker room and bum a cigarette.

The Winners-Tell-Jokes Award to Chuck Daly, coach of the Detroit Pistons. While shopping for a suit, Daly was shown one priced for $1,300. He was told it was made of virgin wool. Daly asked the salesman if he could show him something that cost about $300 that had come from a sheep that had fooled around a little!

The Dietitian's Award to Dan Reeves, coach of the Denver Broncos. Dan had heart surgery just before the season began, yet missed only six days. He's back now and he's feeling great. The secret, he says, is his diet.

"If it tastes good," says Dan, "I spit it out."

THE BEST OF '91

The Best-Tip Award to Lute Olson, basketball coach at Arizona. Lute said you can forget about drawing a foul on Shaquille O'Neal when a team visits LSU. During the last three minutes of the Arizona-LSU game, he said O'Neal could have had a hatchet and a hammer and they would have called a jump ball.

The Oh-What-A-Relief-It-Is Award to Cincinnati Reds' announcer Marty Brennaman. Marty recently underwent throat surgery. He said he's just thankful he didn't wake up talking like Pee Wee Herman.

The Big-Mac-Attack Award to Melvin Turpin, former UK basketball star. When "Dinner Bell" Mel was traded from Cleveland to Utah, he told the Utah reporters on the phone that he weighed 265 pounds. When he arrived in Salt Lake the next day, the Jazz weighed him at 282. Mel looked at the reporters and shrugged, "I like airplane food."

The Chose-The-Wrong-Sport Award to Ray "Rock" Oliver, strength coach for the UK basketball team. Before he came to UK, Rock had always been involved with football. He now admits that he wishes he was still in the pigskin sport.

"In football, all the coaches wear polyester," Rock said. "But now I have to dress like Rick Pitino, and it's costing me a fortune!"

The Sharper-Than-A-Serpent's-Tooth Award to Pat Williams, general manager of the Orlando Magic. Ever since the NBA team signed 300-pound-plus Stanley Roberts, Williams has had a field day at Roberts' expense. Williams says Roberts' idea of a salad is "putting a piece of lettuce on a pizza!"

The Best-Sports-Story Award to David Housel, sports information director at Auburn. Housel wrote a story in one of the Auburn football game programs about two talented Auburn prospects. He wrote that Otto McNabb had all the intangibles to be a great football player and that Joe Mack was a great physical specimen.

Immediately, the story hit the radio talk shows. Callers were begging for more information about the two recruits. Meanwhile, coaches at other Southeastern Conference schools were panicking. They didn't have the slightest idea who McNabb and Mack were.

Auburn, on the other hand, knew that it was against NCAA rules to name recruits. Two SEC schools reported Auburn, and Bob Barrett of the SEC office called the school with a complaint. Associate athletics director Hindman Wall called Housel into his office and told him that since he had broken NCAA rules, the school would have to stop recruiting this dynamic duo.

What everyone didn't know was that Housel had read two books over the summer — James Michener's "Texas" and Louis L'Amour's "Last of the Breed." Otto McNabb and Joe Mack were the main characters in the books. Housel's intent of the story was to show how silly recruiting is to the fans.

As he put it, "I went fishing for brim and I caught a whale!"